rüffer & rub visionaries

Nicole Müller

PATRICK HOHMANN

THE ORGANIC COTTON PIONEER

Translated by Suzanne Kirkbright

The author and the publisher express special thanks for the generous support from

Remei AG

rüffer & rub Sachbuchverlag receives support from the Federal Office of Culture with a structural grant for 2016–2020.

Originally published as
Patrick Hohmann – Der Bio-Baumwollpionier

First edition summer 2019

info@ruefferundrub.ch | www.ruefferundrub.ch

Typeface: Filo Pro
Printing and binding: Book on Demand GmbH, Norderstedt, Germany
Paper: Cream white, 90 g/m^2

ISBN 978-3-906304-57-1

To my beloved Dida,
in gratitude

Foreword

Anne Rüffer, Publisher

2 December 2015, Geneva. An illustrious audience has filled the "Auditorium Ivan Pictet" to celebrate the recent Alternative Nobel Prize Laureates. It is rare for an event's address – the "Maison de la Paix" – to be so unmistakeably well suited to the evening's theme. Germany's Federal Minister for the Environment, Barbara Hendriks, and the Director-General of the UN Office at Geneva, Michael Møller, present the opening speeches under the title theme, "On the Frontlines and in the Courtrooms: Forging Human Security."

The ensuing discussion between the four 2015 prizewinners suddenly features the statement that I find electrifying: "The UN was founded after the Second World War to save forthcoming generations from being hostage to conflict. Since that time there have been more than 170 conflicts – and you never debated the possibility of abolishing wars? Come on, guys, that's just incredible!" Embarrassed laughter and murmurs of astonished disbelief among the audience, but Dr Gino Strada, who is the founder of the international humanitarian organization "Emergency", knows only too well what he is talking about. Since the early 1990s he has set up medical clinics in war-torn regions and provided assistance to the civilian victims – 10% are combatants of the various warring parties and 90% are civilians. He finished his statement with the observation: "Feel free to call me a utopian, because everything is a utopia until somebody puts his idea into practice."

Probably one of the most frequently quoted phrases in recent decades is “I have a dream.” Not only Martin Luther King had a dream, but countless people imagine a fairer world for everyone. Some of these personalities – more than we recognize and by no means enough – turn their dream into reality with dedication, kind-heartedness and wisdom. They are pioneers in their fields; indeed, we may call them utopians – like Gino Strada, Martin Luther King, Mother Teresa or Jody Williams. Nevertheless, every outstanding achievement began with an idea, a hope or a vision.

To capture and convey the spark of an idea, hope or vision and so to ignite a flame of personal dedication is the aim of our new book series – “rüffer&rub visionaries”. At the forefront is the authors’ personal interpretation of their chosen theme. Their intriguing words describe how they became aware of the scientific, cultural or social issue and what motivated their mission to explore well-grounded answers and sustainable solutions. Their inspirational texts illustrate what it means to develop and experience first-hand a personal mission. Whether this is about political, social, scientific or spiritual visions – all the authors share the common yearning for a better world and the willingness to devote their energies fully to this.

Their topics and endeavours may be multifaceted, but their actions are motivated by the deep conviction that it is possible to achieve a better future and a healthy planet for everyone. In this spirit, we believe that each and every one of us can be a part of the solution through our own actions.

Patrick Hohmann and the White Gold

"It cannot be fair for an Indian farmer to subsidize my T-shirt."

It is a cold and windy day in early summer. In the garden of the Tisch + Bar restaurant in the Swiss town of Riesch-Rotkreuz the waitresses snatch at the menus flying about, while the guests weigh down the napkins with their hands to prevent them from fluttering away. A waiter kneels on the ground to sweep up the broken glass shards from the gravel. Patrick Hohmann wants to pay. He leans over the card reader pushed toward him by the waitress and clasps the device in both hands. "I see nothing on it," he says and laughs. The first attempt to leave a tip fails. Hohmann lifts his gaze and blinks up at the waitress's face, dazzled by the light. "I cannot see anything," he says and continues laughing, enthralled like a child jumping over and again into a puddle. The tall man leans over the display once more to type in a tip with his eyes close up to the small payment screen. "Now it has worked," he remarks happily and leans back. Not seeing a thing but having another go; venturing forth into uncertain territory, failing and starting again. Concentrating on one's business, while the whole world rushes off. The microcosm of this scene seems to reveal what defines Patrick Hohmann as an entrepreneur.

Patrick Hohmann is a pioneer of organic cotton. Remei, the company that he founded together with his wife Elisabeth Hohmann Holdener and other friends, is the world's leading supplier of organic cotton. The certified quality labels bioRe®

Sustainable Cotton and bioRe® Textiles, which are produced from the cotton, fulfil five criteria: production is on fair terms, carbon neutral, ecological and gentle to the skin. Lastly, full transparency applies for the complete production chain. Consumers can use a digital app to check each supplier, so the entire production line is retraceable back to the farmer who sowed, nurtured and harvested the cotton.

Patrick Hohmann regards the business model he has developed as the outcome of simple logic. He is a qualified textile engineer who takes it for granted that we should not recklessly harm nature, which sustains livelihoods for all people, no matter which continent they live on. In his view, reason is at the heart of a sense of community that is in the balance. Discrimination against others and the challenges of globalization, which impose unfair risks on those who experience poverty – such aspects are entirely illogical. "It cannot be fair for an Indian farmer to subsidize my T-shirt," asserts Hohmann.

Until the 1990s Patrick Hohmann was a yarn and cotton dealer like many others. However, one day Hohmann began a conversation with an Indian cotton farmer: "I wanted to know how much he earns. About one US dollar per kilogram. And how much of this did he invest in chemicals? – 70 cents. A further 70 cents are spent on chemicals because the state subsidizes the use of pesticides by up to 50%. Who is the farmer working for? He has no contact with the dealer or the customer; he produces in a vacuum and yet he still gets into debt." Hohmann can no longer forget such economic absurdity. How can a product incurring production costs of more than USD 1.40 only bring in one dollar? Besides, how do agricultural workers earn next to nothing, while at the other end of the production chain, i.e. with ready-to-wear clothing, the profits virtually flow in?

One must bear in mind how much cotton matters in our society to appreciate Patrick Hohmann's singular lifetime achievement. Everyday items are a case in point, and you will be amazed how ubiquitous the textile is. We wear T-shirts, blouses and shirts; we pull on jeans and cotton socks. Babies lie on cotton towels clenching hold of their cotton comforters in their tiny fists. Perfect damask tablecloths decorate restaurant tables. We sleep under duvets with cotton covers and we pull curtains – all of them are made from 100 % cotton. Apart from these fabrics, which we instantly notice, cotton is hidden in some surprising things like banknotes or coffee filters. Even the product marketed as 'vegetable oil' is invariably nothing more than cottonseed oil.

The Harvard historian Sven Beckert's comprehensive and enthralling book "Empire of Cotton" pays homage to the history of cotton. Beckert shows how cotton stirred the industrial revolution and bestowed great prosperity on Europe. Until 1760 most Europeans wore garments made from linen and wool, while the upper classes perhaps wore silk. These materials were itchy, heavy to wash and dyeing them was complicated. The world of our ancestors was – apart from the bright churches and beautifully decorated country manors – colourless and there were some strong odours. That changed fundamentally due to the importance of cotton.

Beckert's statistical research shows that globalization, as we know it, was initiated, sustained and made profitable due to cotton. The profound gap that nowadays divides the global North from the global South is basically related to the 19th-century cotton industry. Unlike other commodities, such as rice or tobacco, cotton is processed in two intensive phases: work on the fields and in the factories. Cotton must be ginned (deseeded) and the lint pressed into bales; its fibres must be spun into yarn. Cotton yarn must be woven into the textile, which is knitted or crocheted, depending on whether the design is for a jersey fitted sheet or a light summer jumper. Finally, the fabrics must be dyed and finished.

The inventive talent of the technically skilled Europeans and Americans, and their spirit of enlightenment were not the only factors that turned Manchester, Mulhouse (Alsace) or Lowell in Massachusetts into centres of international commerce. The incentive was rather what Beckert calls "war capitalism": the violent and compulsory acquisition of land and the slavery of people in Asia, Africa and the two Americas. War capitalism first divided the world into an agricultural sector and a production sector. The cotton industry connected extremely remote regions and merged them together with a common destiny. "Cotton provides the key to understanding the modern world, the great inequalities that characterize it, the long history of globalization, and the ever-changing political economy of capitalism,"[1] explains the historian Beckert.

For centuries, Indian smallholders had cultivated cotton for their own purposes. Their cloths, which they wove on the handloom, were intended for their personal use and at best for conveyance to local rulers. After the industrial revolution, i.e. following the advent of the machine age at the turn of the 19th and 20th centuries, the Indian markets were swamped with cheap, machine-produced cotton textiles from Europe, mainly from England. This halted the development opportunities for Indian commerce; the farmers were forced to work on the fields. It is no coincidence that Mahatma Ghandi made the hand-spun fabric of the *khadi* a symbol of non-violent resistance against the British. He proudly wore the traditional, hand-woven garment called the dhoti and encouraged his fellow countrymen to wear local fabrics. In doing so, he showed Indians a way of refusing to consent to their own repression. Ghandi's non-violent resistance was successful: his original design with a spinning wheel forms part of the Indian flag today.

During the 19th and early 20th centuries when workers began to resist the noisy, smoke-filled factories in Europe and to demand higher wages and social welfare benefits, the textile industry slowly returned to Asia and Africa. Today, at regular intervals the textile-producing countries are shocked by scandals that also instil in us a vague sense of powerlessness. On 24 April 2013 the collapse of a garment factory in Bangladesh, crushing and killing 1,135 people, sent a wave of outrage around the world.

At the same time, the reports showed that it was not so easy to find those who were culpable because of the immense power concentrated in the system that often left individuals feeling helpless.

The cotton industry is a global business worth billions; it depends on labour specialization and a high degree of differentiation and it relies on countless regulatory adjustments and parameters that the average person who loves to wear T-shirts is entirely ignorant about. Cotton is usually grown and harvested in regions with weak infrastructure. A reliable supply of electricity is mostly lacking here. The raw cotton is transported and the respective region is deprived of the opportunity to participate in the cotton added value chain. Ginning the raw cotton, spinning the fibres to yarn and weaving are all work phases that occur elsewhere, at a considerable distance from where the sun's rays first touched the cotton. The natural commodity is frequently transported to another country for processing. The cotton industry is a nomadic business that follows the trail of the cheapest price. If Tanzanian cotton is cheaper to spin in Zambia, then it is transported to Zambia, even though Tanzania has spinning mills that could accept the work.

The purchasers of cotton products act globally. But the suppliers depend on local conditions. It is perfectly plausible for a government in country A to raise the minimum price for cotton with the aim of generating supplementary revenue for local farmers. However, if the global purchasers can procure the same type of cotton more cheaply in country B, then the farmers in country A not only make no supplementary income, but rather they earn nothing at all. The system is fragile and complicated. The fact that the cotton price is fixed in US dollars also exposes the farmers to significant risks. The yield and quality can be good, but if the American dollar is devalued, then the farmers earn less money in real terms in their local currency. The systemic risks are compounded by dependency on the weather, a factor that becomes progressively more acute during climate change.

"The consumer wears cotton, or buys carrots and has no idea what this actually involves," remarks Patrick Hohmann. If you want more informed insights, you are swiftly confronted with some disconcerting facts. About 200 million people earn their livelihood directly or indirectly from cotton, from planting the cotton or from downstream work processes. The big players in the cultivation of cotton are India, China and the US. Brazil, Pakistan and Turkey rank fifth, sixth and seventh. Of the annual 80-million tonne cotton harvest only a vanishingly small amount is organic cotton, that is, an estimated 1%. Today, the conventional way of farming cotton is a disaster for humans and the environment. Thirty years ago, the Aral Sea, which belongs to Uzbekistan and Kazakhstan, was the size of Bavaria. What once was a lake has now practically dried out, and all that remains is a toxic, dusty salt desert, a consequence of the pesticides used in cotton farming in Uzbekistan. Soviet engineers developed an elaborate irrigation system to divert water from the 30-metre deep lake, because it takes between 10,000 and

20,000 litres of water to produce one kilogram of cotton. In areas lacking in natural rainfall, the result is immense environmental damage, which causes the world's climate to worsen and affect us all. Water is not the only problem. The harm done to the 'green lung' is also among the consequences of industrial-scale cotton farming. In Brazil, every year thousands of hectares of rainforest are cut and cleared in order to plant cotton.

One of the bitter ironies of the cotton industry is that environmental sins go hand in hand with growing poverty for the people who cultivate the cotton. For instance, China, the world's biggest cotton producer, must permanently buy up and hoard gargantuan quantities of cotton so that state intervention measures protect its domestic producers. The cotton is removed from the market to create an artificial shortage and maintain price stability. US subsidy policies also distort the market. Up till 2014 American cotton farmers received more in subsidies than their revenue from sales of the commodity. When Brazil started legal proceedings against the US for these trade violations, the United States had to pay a fine of USD 300 million and cancel the subsidies to its farmers in Texas, Georgia, Arkansas, Mississippi and California. However, nothing has really changed. The cotton farmers continue to receive state support with deficit guarantees, or compensation payments opaquely masquerading as support for hurricane victims, and with massively discounted insurance premiums for crop failure. Yet, it is not as though American cotton farmers are especially well off. Many of them only make ends meet with a second income, an additional job somewhere in the city. They are also victims of a market that no longer forms genuine pricing. Many of them would prefer to pull out of cotton, but they have accrued debts from a pool of machinery that can only be used to harvest cotton. An automated machine for the cotton harvest easily costs

USD 750,000 – at the same time, monocultures offer little flexibility. Besides, cotton farmers have employees on the payroll, people for whom they feel responsible. Moreover, always relying on the drip-feed of tax payer subsidies must be depressing as well as creating a product that makes no real profit.

Presently, no exact statistics are available about how much of the total volume of farmed cotton is transgenic crop. The share is calculated as 64–81%, depending on the source.[2] Every year, an estimated 51 million tonnes to 65 million tonnes of raw cotton are genetically modified. In other words, the genetic material of the cotton plant has been manipulated with a protein that kills or should kill the classic cotton pests. Unless you have made a conscious choice to purchase clothes made from organic cotton, as you read these lines, you will be wearing a garment made from GM cotton. In practice, during the first three or four years, the yield of genetically modified hybrid plants is actually higher and there is a reduction in the use of pesticides. However, after this interval the pests develop resistance and this means using stronger pesticides in even bigger doses, even more genetic modification, even more aggressive pesticides and so forth. GM seeds are also patented. Last but not least, the seeds that are produced from a genetically modified plant can only germinate to a limited extent. The idea behind this is that every year the farmer must purchase new seed and so money flows into the coffers of the giant corporations. Swissaid estimates that now three agricultural companies own about two-thirds of all cotton seeds. This is not only a dangerous curtailment of biodiversity, but also an existential threat for farmers.

"The sewers and seamstresses are underpaid," comments Patrick Hohmann, "but farming is even lower paid." Smallholders in poor countries have no savings. Therefore, they buy bulk quantities of seeds and pesticides. Of course, they hope that selling the harvest will earn enough money to cover the costs. If something happens – a pest infestation, adverse weather, a water shortage – the debt trap slams shut. Every year Indian daily newspapers like the “Times of India” or “The Hindu” publish reports about a group of farmers’ suicides in rural areas. Although the tone of the articles is quite sympathetic, they rarely shed light on the actual circumstances.

A lone individual can circulate abundant and paltry facts at the same time. When Patrick Hohmann stands on a station platform somewhere, he is just one passer-by among the countless commuters. He is a tall, broad-shouldered, friendly-looking man in an anorak and chinos, with a rucksack slung over one shoulder. He has dedicated half of his professional life to improving the lot of farmers and producing cotton in a way that is kind and not harmful to nature. Nevertheless, the business model he has developed in conjunction with his partners over many years leads to repeated challenges and adjustments. The production processes of bioRe® Sustainable Cotton & Textiles are exposed to the enormous pressure forces and dominance of an industry which puts profitable returns first. Resisting the allure of profit maximization calls for human empathy, courage and a great deal of ingenuity of the kind that helped David win victory against Goliath.

Patrick Hohmann has accepted responsibility and put this commitment into practice in the cotton industry. This is undoubtedly impressive, but it is just one small element of what makes him such an inspirational presence. Hohmann is a business artist. If you trace his lifetime achievement, the most amazing attributes are chiefly the mix of sober analysis, creativity and skilful mathematics, bone-dry technical knowledge and an urge to experiment. He is an accountant and philosopher rolled into one. The unequivocal acceptance of difficulties has made him a successful entrepreneur. "Nowhere is it written that life should be easy. Life is always being a little lucky and a little unlucky," according to Patrick Hohmann's insight as an entrepreneur. He knows that his achievement is always fragile and mutable. What inspires this pioneer is a positive attitude of dealing with agile, fast-moving scenarios and an ability to react in a measured way. He is creative and finely attuned to the needs of humans, animals and nature.

Patrick Hohmann and his team refuse to be disheartened. They contrast a largely faceless system with trust in the humane individual. It is clear that powerful people will not save us. Pioneers like Patrick Hohmann or films like "Tomorrow" and "Fair Traders" highlight how change begins on a small scale, as a 'grassroots' movement, which can motivate and inspire others. Innovation almost always springs up at society's margins. It evolves gradually, often out of sight, spurred on by individuals, who are dissatisfied with the status quo and want to pursue new approaches. "You may say he's a dreamer," one could describe Patrick Hohmann as a variation of John Lennon's song. "But he's not the only one." It takes good fortune as well as other people who are willing to take responsibility, so innovative ideas can gravitate from society's margins to its epicentre. Before you know it, you will shake your head in recollection of what you willingly accepted as 'normal' till recently.

"A system resolution only happens when the system has become redundant," Patrick Hohmann once stated. This was one of those sayings that he casually threw into the conversation, and you only appreciate its importance much later. It is worthwhile reflecting on this phrase for a while longer.

FROM SEEDS TO READY-TO-WEAR FASHION

Protracted timescales. And several continents. The path from cotton cultivation to the finished garment is incredibly long, with many specialist work phases. Growing the organic cotton is just the start. Patrick Hohmann and his company Remei as well as the bioRe® foundations have taken great efforts to establish the entire supply chain based on the following criteria:

- organic cotton
- fair production
- ecological and gentle on the skin
- CO_2-neutral
- re-traceable back to the farmer

Countless official adjustments and parameters can influence the supply chain. These include climatic and cultural conditions, regulatory guidelines, infrastructure and innovations, trends and last but not least the willingness of consumers to understand complicated processes and to support these financially and based on truthful ideals. Close partnerships and mutual understanding are essential to create fashion whose production is kind, and not harmful to humans and nature.

Advance payment

Smallholders in Tanzania and India generally struggle with cash shortfalls. Pay day is only once a year, at harvest time. bioRe® handles advance payments with interest-free loans or the supply of seeds on a commission basis. bioRe® also bears the risk of overproduction. The 80% purchase guarantee ensures that farmers avoid non-supply of their product. This relieves pressure on their families and helps them to improve planning.

Seed research

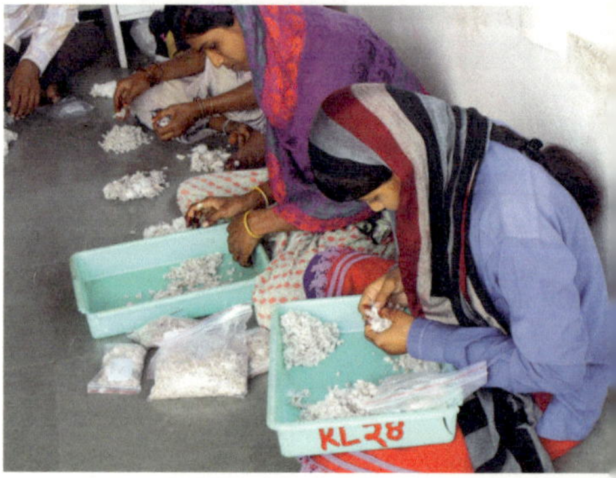

bioRe® India runs a state-recognized research institute and invests in seed research. In India, as most cotton is genetically modified, non-GMO seeds are no longer available in sufficient quantities. By 2020 bioRe® will be able to offer large quantities of GMO-free seeds, including natural hybrid varieties, which give extremely high yields.

Sowing

Cotton sowing occurs before the rainy season, in May or June in India, and in November, December and January in Tanzania. Line sowing is done by hand or with a sowing machine. The bioRe® cotton crop is planted in rotation to enable the soil to recover. Rotation crops planted after the cotton harvest include vegetables, pulses, millet or maize.

Plant protection and manures

bioRe® cotton is cultivated without chemical and synthetic pesticides and without gene technology. Beneficial insects are used and natural organic manures, like a brew made from neem leaves. Another method is to bury in the ground soil-filled cow horns from biodynamic farming. Other measures to prevent soil erosion include natural hedges.

Growth

Cotton needs plenty of water. Between 10,000 to 20,000 litres are required to produce 1 kilogram of cotton. During the rainy season – as long as climate change does not disrupt the seasonal cycle – there is sufficient water to ensure that the plant grows at a fast pace.

Harvest

The women usually walk along the rows of plants and pick the cotton bolls. The opened capsules are dry and pointed at the tips; the harvesters must take care to avoid minor injuries. The plucked cotton bolls contain fluffy cotton seeds.

Gathering

The farmers gather the cotton on their fields and pack it inside bed sheets. Everyone is nervous about the harvest all year round, worrying and hoping that everything will go well. A good yield relieves the pressure on families and lightens the mood.

Transport

bioRe® operates central warehouses and collection centres to accept the cotton. The farmers use their own vehicles to bring their harvest here. Most farmers transport the cotton with an ox cart. In exceptional cases the harvest is also collected.

Collection centres

The quality of the accepted cotton is checked and the volume is weighed. Cotton with a 'pink bollworm' infestation shows some yellowness and the fibres are damaged. At the collection centres the cotton is packed into sacks and prepared for onward transport.

Ginning

In the ginning unit the seeds are combed out of the white bolls using automated gins with spiked cylinders that separate the seeds. The end products are the pressed raw cotton bolls and seeds that can be re-used during the next sowing season. Cotton seeds can also be pressed and used in cottonseed oil. Compliance with production conditions and social standards involves continual monitoring. Constructive cooperation is promoted by regular visits and partnership development initiatives.

Spinning

Due to poor infrastructure (electricity, spare parts, specialist staff etc.) the cotton is usually spun into yarn far away from the growing area. The firmness and thickness of the yarn already determines whether it is then knit into fine jersey or a heavier knitted fabric. Remei controls yarn production and ensures that yarn is available at several worldwide locations for seamless production. Monitoring also applies in this phase for compliance with production and social conditions.

Design

The collections are created at Remei AG's headquarters in Rotkreuz, Switzerland. The designer devises the full collections or single garments in consultation with the purchasers for the relevant trading brand and in line with their preferences, e.g. Coop. Meeting the standards of bioRe® Sustainable Textiles must already be integrated at the design stage, which is an important step to a clean textile.

Fabric production

The bioRe® organic cotton is processed into knitted fabric in Lithuania and India using state-of-the-art machines. Remei manufactures no woven fabrics, since the volumes would be too great for Remei's current market. However, bioRe® yarns are also sold to Japan, where textiles made from organic cotton are created for the Japanese market.

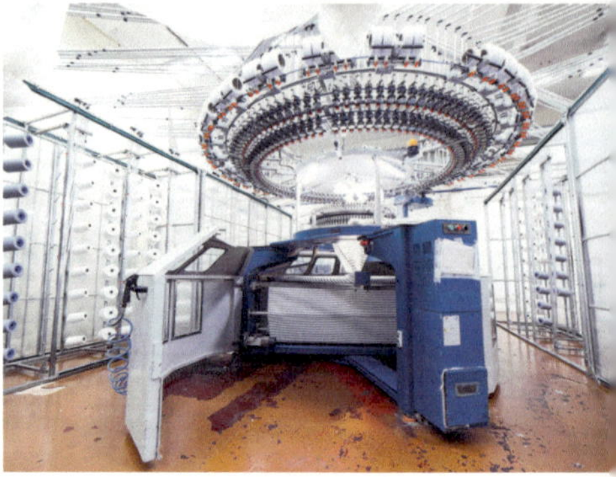

Dyeing

Dyeing occurs without the addition of toxins and waste water is cleaned. Monitoring also applies here for compliance with controlled production and social standards. The continual improvement of processes is thanks to regular visits and constant dialogue with the production partners.

Cut

A handful of SA8000-certified production sites make the finished bioRe® garments. Direct contact between Remei and the production partners is the basis for assuring production and the constant development of the textile products. Personal contact with production partners is an absolute one-off in the textile sector.

Ready-to-wear

The factories that finish bioRe® clothing are SA8000-certified. The sewers and seamstresses earn wages that guarantee their livelihoods, and they can have a say with the help of worker representatives. The agreed production conditions and social standards are monitored. Ecological standards apply for printing and embroidering, and these are regularly monitored. The printing pastes and pigments are safe and the same applies for the appliqué embroidery threads.

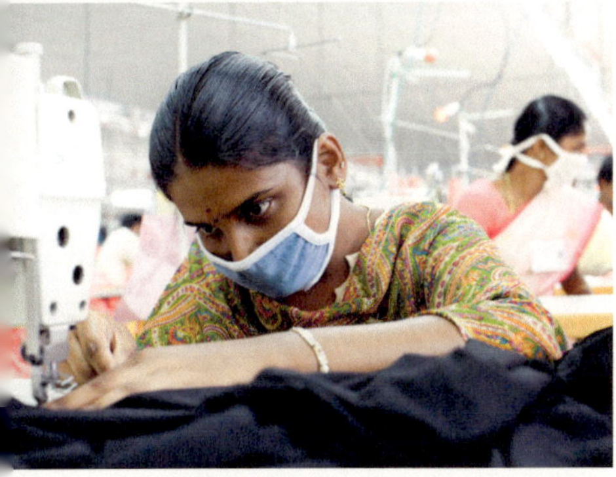

Collections

The label bioRe® Sustainable Textiles sets the highest organic cotton standard worldwide for the holistic connection of ecology and social standards. So far, it is the only label to assure and guarantee in practice that high ethical and ecological values apply for the entire textile supply chain – from cotton fibre to the finished garment.

The bioRe® brand sets trends for decision-makers in the textile trade and end consumers and has potential for identification – upgrade your style.

Geo-tracking

The strict controls assured by the company internally and with the certifying agencies are fully re-traceable for the consumers. bioRe® products have a traceability number that, thanks to a traceability app, you can photograph and input with your smartphone. A list displays all the factories that participate in the production process. There are no supplier secrets because we openly encourage others to follow our example.

Childhood in Alexandria

"I followed a calling at a very young age."

Undoubtedly, Patrick Hohmann's mother was the driving force in his family. Ellen Hohmann, née Collins, was born in 1920 in the French town of Bar-sur-Aube. Her father, Charles Collins, was an Irish immigrant to America who held a British passport. During the First World War, Collins had to return to Europe to fight under the British flag. At that time, Ireland had still not gained independence but was part of the United Kingdom. When Collins fell in love with the Frenchwoman Annemarie Thierry, he got married and stayed in Bar-sur-Aube until the outbreak of the Second World War.

The blood of the revolution flowed in Ellen Hohmann Collins's veins. Among her ancestors was Daniel O'Connell (1775–1847) who has a street named after him in almost every small Irish town. O'Connell was a freedom fighter who strove for and achieved equal status for Catholics and Protestants. He also campaigned for equal rights for farmers and Jews. Daniel O'Connell's second major concern as a Member of Parliament in Britain was the dissolution of the union of Great Britain and Ireland. He was a leading and popular politician who believed in mass demonstrations and non-violent resistance. Unfortunately, his prophecy that this battle would culminate in a violent end, if the British ruling class failed to alter their attitude in time, turned out to be true.

Ellen Collins was a tall, extremely intelligent and attractive young woman who immediately opposed the Nazis when they came to power in Europe. She applied to the Royal Air Force while she was still under age, yet she could not take up the position because her father refused to grant his signature. Ireland had by now gained independence, and her father held the opinion that no member of the Collins clan should fight voluntarily under the British flag.

When the Germans began the blitzkrieg in spring 1940 and occupied France, the family escaped on the last ship to Dover, and from here to London. Ellen Collins had now come of age. She re-applied for the position of teletypist to the Royal Air Force; and she was accepted. She was already on board ship bound for Palestine to start her job there, when bombardments commenced in the region. The ship was diverted, finally landing in Alexandria, Egypt.

Patrick Hohmann's father has an entirely different biography. Gerhart Wilhelm Hohmann, born in 1910, was an orphan and came from a modest background. His father died of heart failure in 1926. His mother contracted tuberculosis shortly afterwards and also died.

Gerhard was the oldest of four brothers. His guardian organized lodgings with a family, so that he could finish his salesman's apprenticeship. His brothers were housed in the orphanage. Gerhart Hohmann passed his apprenticeship examinations with such glowing results that he was immediately offered employment with Reinhart AG in Winterthur. The company was a household name particularly because of the patronage of its founders. The Reinhart Collection and its precious artworks housed in Winterthur are internationally renowned as an outstanding art treasure. Less well known is that to this day the company is one of the leading worldwide cotton

P. 34 | **Patrick Hohmann's father Gerhart Hohmann was already a cotton dealer in Egypt and Sudan.**

Top left | **Patrick Hohmann as a school pupil of the monastery in Einsiedeln.**

Top right | **Patrick Hohmann as a child, together with his young brother Kevin.**

Middle | **Ellen Hohmann Collins, Patrick Hohmann's mother.**

Bottom | **Patrick Hohmann with a sheep.**

merchants: 5–6% of the total annual cotton production continues to be sourced and supplied by Reinhart AG in Winterthur.

The role with Reinhart AG proved fortuitous for Gerhart Hohmann. In 1929 the young salesman was offered a job with prospects: he could work as Albert Reinhart's personal secretary either in India or Egypt. Hohmann chose Egypt, as it was easier travelling back from here to Switzerland to visit his brothers who still lived in the orphanage. In 1949 – by now, he had worked his way up as a full-time cotton trader for Reinhart – Gerhart Hohmann became a partner in Escher AG, a cotton trading company with headquarters in Egypt. Ultimately, he took over ownership of the business.

Patrick Hohmann's parents' marriage was like fire and water. On the one hand, his father was quiet, hard-working and conscientious and had a strong appetite for adventure. If his wife had not stopped him, Gerhart Hohmann would not have hesitated to paddle solo in a folding canoe along the White Nile. On the other hand, Ellen Hohmann Collins was a status-conscious, vivacious woman from a good family. After enduring long nights in the bomb shelter during the air raids in London, she felt a subtle disdain for the Swiss, who were spared the conflict. Ellen Hohmann Collins confidently participated in the social circles in Alexandria, and her husband approved of this. She had impeccable manners and was witty and educated. In Egypt, she began to take an interest in archaeology, the only hobby that equally inspired both her and her husband. Ellen Hohmann Collins reportedly had an awkward personality. She did not find it easy to show appreciation for other people's achievements. She had fixed views about how things should be. There was no scope for negotiation. She cajoled her husband – as a stubborn Irish woman – throughout his life, urging him to convert to Catholicism. Gerhart Hohmann remained a Protestant, but did agree to a Catholic upbringing for his sons.

Patrick Hans Hohmann was born in 1950 in Alexandria as the second of three sons. In 1947 Charles Gerhart was born, and in 1955 Kevin Heinrich arrived as the last of the brothers. The sons all have English first names with a German middle name, because their father Gerhart Hohmann had the notion that English names might later prevent his sons from pursuing careers in the Swiss military. What is more, their mother was insistent about the revolutionary legacy of her family heritage. She was keen for her sons to be called O'Connell, though the Swiss passport system made no provision for this. Ellen Hohmann quickly smuggled 'O'Connell' into the papers, as her sons' third first names, which are still there in black and white.

Alexandria in the 1940s and 1950s was an exciting place filled with music, colours and aromas. The city had over a million inhabitants with kilometre-long, light sandy beaches and a bustling port that was an important international trading centre, especially for oil and cotton. The city was home to large communities of widely diverse nationalities. Dual citizenship was permitted, which attracted many migrants from Spain, Greece and Italy, including many Jews. However, Patrick Hohmann hardly experienced any of the liveliness of his birthplace. "We led a fairly isolated life," he recalls. The Hohmanns lived in a colonial style villa with a large garden, surrounded by a high wall. The children were not allowed to leave the garden. Patrick was indifferent about this. "When my parents had their siesta, I climbed up one of the trees and watched the builders who were working on the other side of the wall. One of them saw me and invited me to join them. I jumped down and had a cup of tea with them," recounts Hohmann and adds wistfully, "I followed a calling at a very young age."

This remark about a calling gives an indication of the spiritual attitude that epitomizes Patrick Hohmann's entrepreneurial activity. Hohmann is convinced through his work as an organic cotton dealer that we all shoulder responsibility for a task; we are born with a vocation. While we may be oblivious about this, we gradually come to appreciate and hopefully embrace it. In Patrick Hohmann's view, everyone intuitively follows such a calling. Something pulls at the soul, without us even knowing what it is. We have an inkling of what we can do and what we are born to achieve in the light of personal experience, through failure and by starting from scratch. "I didn't jump over the wall because I wanted to, but because I can. I have always been interested in what lies behind the border, and what goes on there when you cross the border."

A nanny looked after the children while they were at home. As soon as they had to attend school, their father drove his sons in the Chevrolet to the French-speaking Swiss school, where they had to swot up on oral and written Arabic. During the never-ending journeys, Hohmann senior practised with his boys an essential skill for a cotton merchant, namely, mental arithmetic.

These years were marked by two influences that shaped Patrick Hohmann's later life: being a refugee and the experience of culture shock.

On 30 July 1956 the Egyptian President Gamal Abdel Nasser announced the nationalization of the Suez Canal Company that was under French and British ownership. France, Great Britain and Israel attacked Egypt. The crisis was described in the American media as "the biggest threat this year has posed to world peace." The Hohmann family packed their suitcases and fled to Sudan. "Nowadays, when you hear the word 'refugee', perhaps you think of events in Syria or the Mediterranean. But it wasn't so dramatic. When we were children, it primarily meant that our parents only spoke to each other in whispers. And it meant travelling on an endlessly long train journey across the desert. Sometimes, the train stopped in the middle of the desert, until somebody with a hammer turned up again and repaired the train," Patrick Hohmann describes these unsettling days.

In Khartoum, Sudan's capital city, the parents at least felt a sense of release from the tension and the immediate pressure abated. The family had contacts here; waiting at the station to collect them was Kevin Hayes, who was a cousin of grandfather Charles Collins. Kevin Hayes, who is also Patrick Hohmann's godfather, was a magistrate of the British Empire in Khartoum.

At first, the family lived in the beautiful Grand Hotel, a time-honoured colonial building. Patrick Hohmann especially remembers one anecdote: "Every morning, I pilfered the leftover bread rolls from the tables to take them to the hippopotamus in the neighbouring zoo. You only had to call the animal by name, then it opened its mouth. Bintifatma, eftach, eftach!"

The conflict in Egypt carried on, and the parents wanted to get their sons to safety. First, they sent Charles and one-year-old Kevin back to Switzerland, where they were both accepted at the Bosshard boarding school and children's home in Aegeri. Patrick Hohmann, who was suffering from inflammation of the knee and wearing a leg splint, moved with his parents to Port Sudan, where the Hohmanns occupied a modest room in the Red Sea Hotel. For a short while, he was also sent somewhere safe: he spent the summer of 1957 with his maternal grandparents on the Ile de Dieu in Brittany. Afterwards, he and his parents returned once again to Alexandria. In 1961, five years after the start of the Suez Crisis, his father's firm, Escher AG, was nationalized. Now, Gerhart Hohmann was increasingly trading in cotton from Sudan. He was not spared a takeover of his business for a second time, in 1971, and on this occasion in Sudan.

Patrick Hohmann was eleven years old in 1961, the year of the nationalization. It was a turbulent time. A number of North African states were fighting for their independence. Renowned for its brutality, the Algerian war was raging in the country when the colonial power, France, reacted with extreme harshness against the independence attempts. In Yemen, there were attacks on the British occupiers. Both countries, Algeria and Yemen, were supported by Egypt and its president Gamal Abdel Nasser. In this tense situation, the Hohmanns also decided to send their second-born son to boarding school in Switzerland. Charles, Patrick's three-year older brother, was already attending the Pfister boarding school in Oberägeri.

Patrick Hohmann's parents took him to the airport. The child travelled all alone from Egypt to Zurich-Kloten where he was collected by his godmother Margrit Hefti. Two days later, Patrick Hohmann continued the journey to Celerina, where without speaking a word of German he was to learn the language and prepare to attend the monastery school in Einsiedeln.

Together with other pupils, and accompanied by the headmaster of the Albris Institute, he was travelling to an unknown, alien world. For Patrick Hohmann, it was an obvious turning point. "When I tell this story today, it seems terrible to me, but at the time it's just how it was. You adapted to the situation. In Egypt, everything was bright, sunny and blue sky. Suddenly, everything was dark. We travelled by train to Celerina through the Via Mala. Everyone was enthusiastic, only I felt things closing in on me and I thought: how do I just get out of here again? It rained constantly; at supper time, there was dark hot chocolate and the chalets were jet-black. Within the first three days I already watched as a few pupils beat up a schoolmate. I thought: my goodness, what if this also happens to me! I immediately tried to fit into the community and to find a way of getting on with the others." Patrick Hohmann would only see his brothers and parents twice or three times a year in subsequent years – at Christmas and Easter, and occasionally for holidays together.

Saying goodbye to the Arabic world must have been an exceptionally painful experience for the boy whom his classmates in Celerina only called the "Egyptian". However, Patrick Hohmann also associates this experience with something positive: in Celerina, he learned to hold his own as an exotic stranger in a strict environment, which was dominated by prejudices. He came to terms with the situation and tried to make the best of things. "My ability," explains Hohmann, "to cope with difficulties, to take an interest in others and always to look forwards, stems from that time."

Patrick Hohmann stayed in Celerina for one-and-a-half years. When he transferred to Einsiedeln, the feeling of being hemmed in intensified. The daily routine followed a strict pattern. The pupils, who had to wear black gowns, were practically under house arrest; they were not allowed to leave the monastery. Even sports activities took place inside the monastery walls. For the freedom-loving boy, who was reading Karl May and dreaming of wide-open prairies, who enjoyed playing football and skiing, it was torturous at Einsiedeln. Now, he was supposed to swot up on Latin and ancient Greek as well, and he had only just learned German. "I wasn't interested in these dead languages," remarks Hohmann. "I'm somebody who prefers to get on with things." When his grades worsened, his mother and the fathers finally understood and allowed him to transfer to a different school. At the Kollegium Schwyz, Hohmann studied for the Swiss Matura (type C) school-leaving certificate, whose primary focus was mathematics and the natural sciences, including physics and modern languages. Life at the boarding school in Canton Schwyz was also Catholic and spartan. Roberto Müller, whom Hohmann got to know at the 'Kollegi' and who remains a close friend, described it as follows: "More than one hundred pupils slept in a large dormitory, you can imagine how that smelled. We showered once a week, it was hot water for five minutes and then it turned cold with the shout, 'Attention, cold!' In the lower classes we were never allowed to go out! You felt on top of the world during a walk on Sunday afternoon with the deputy prefect at the head of the line." Hohmann suffered less than his friend due to the house rules. He arranged little escapes for himself, by obtaining a moped, which he hid in the shrubbery of a garden. Of course, Hohmann also signed up for the theatre course, because that was the opportunity to make contact with girls. The charming young man was popular with the girls – more girls than the fathers would have liked. At this age, as the fathers updated his mother, one girlfriend was fine, but several girlfriends at the same time, that was going too far. The fathers could not know that soon, even before finishing his Matura exam in 1970, Patrick Hohmann was to meet the woman who still shares his life today.

In the Shadow of the "Pfullingen Underpants"

"One morning, my mother woke me and said, 'Here, I have something for you.'"

Patrick Hohmann was not exactly a brilliant pupil; he scraped through his Matura school-leaving certificate from the Kollegium Schwyz. He could excel in mathematics, physics and both his native languages English and French, yet only if he liked the teacher. He was indifferent to other linguistic subjects. He didn't know what he wanted to do after leaving school. However, he had a clear idea of what he preferred not to do – anything but long-winded studies at the ETH Zurich. As far as he was concerned, he had spent long enough in the classroom. Unlike his brother Charles, who was studying humanities in Fribourg, and his younger brother Kevin, who was reading law at the University of Zurich, he was attracted to a practical career. He wanted to be free and to start earning his own money as quickly as possible.

One morning after his exams had finished, his mother came to his bedside and woke him. Ellen Hohmann Collins had found something in the newspaper that she thought was suitable for her son.

"I have something for you," she said. "Textile engineer."

"How long does that take then?"

"Three years, plus one year work experience."

Hohmann suddenly woke up, "Perfect. And where?"

"In Reutlingen," replied his mother. "With the Nazis, but not too far away from Switzerland."

Mother and son were equally delighted at the thought of his studying in Reutlingen, though for different reasons. While his mother hoped to drive a wedge between her son and his new girlfriend, whom she found unsuitable, Patrick Hohmann entertained very different ideas: he would be away from home, though not too far to stop him from visiting Elisabeth Holdener whom he had met at a dancing event. He borrowed his mother's car, smuggled Elisabeth into the vehicle and immediately sped off to Reutlingen to enrol for the study course. "Was someone else in the car?" asked his mother when he returned. "No," lied the son, and 50 years later he is still amazed about his youthful insolence. Hohmann laughs. "In the old days, you could drive as fast as you wanted, but sex before marriage, that was bad. Today, it's the other way around: sex before marriage is no problem, but woe betide you, if you're speeding in the car!"

Reutlingen is not the most attractive destination. The city in Baden-Württemberg now has about 117,000 inhabitants. Situated on a flat peninsula, the city has no obvious limits and sprawls at the foot of the local hill, the Achalm. The region's only landmark is Schönberg Tower, aptly nicknamed by the locals as the "Pfullingen Underpants". The architectural monument on the upper plain of the Schönberg appears from afar like freshly starched underwear.

Reutlingen's city centre has been sympathetically restored; the pedestrian zone is lined with quaint, medieval-looking Swabian häusle. H&M, McDonald's, Apollo Optik, and the usual ensemble, dominate the scene. Outside the city centre, lots of traffic crawls along the narrow streets. Bordering on the motorways are disused industrial sites from the heyday of the textile industry, now having attracted new occupants. Along the small River Echaz, one industrial building proudly follows the next, and there is the occasional saw-tooth roof of the shed warehouses, the hollow structures of bygone greatness. Where currently cat food and children's garden swings are on sale was the former site of pioneering innovations for the textile industry and the associated machinery industry. Reutlingen was one of Europe's leading industrial regions for almost a century. The legendary MT3, the first machine with self-changing tools, was developed in Reutlingen. Its machining tolerance of 0.03 mm was sensational. The left/left knitting machine, which produced exceptionally fine knitwear, was also invented in Reutlingen by the company H. Stoll AG. This was innovative machine engineering, innovation in knitwear and the manufacture of brand-new fabrics. "The fabrics for the Olympic team showcased Reutlingen's reputation around the world," recalls Lothar Kittel, who is a guide at Reutlingen's industrial museum. His words convey a sense of nostalgia and pride.

Patrick Hohmann studied at the Technikum für Textilindustrie, established in 1855. For a while, the attractive red-brick building with adjacent workshops was known as the "royal Technikum". The institution had an excellent reputation and attracted students from all over the world. In 1971, when Hohmann began his studies, the college was undergoing transformation into a technical college. This meant that chemistry and business administration were taught in addition to technological subjects. It also meant that the students had to attain higher standards.

Only thirteen of roughly 40 students who enrolled with Hohmann graduated with diplomas.

Patrick Hohmann was happy. He enjoyed his studies, particularly the vocational part. His chosen specialist subject was spinning technology. It suited him to lie under a machine with a spanner, surrounded by the smell of engine oil and the noise of the clattering machines. However, something happened in his second semester that neither he nor his girlfriend had anticipated: Elisabeth Holdener became pregnant. She had yet to graduate from the teacher training college at the Theresianum in Ingenbohl near Brunnen. Both families were upset. Armin Holdener, Elisabeth's father, who actually liked his daughter's boyfriend, was angry with Patrick Hohmann. "Young man, don't think that I'm proud of you!" he exclaimed and shook his index finger so fiercely that the father-to-be could no longer see his finger. An illegitimate grandchild, while his daughter was still studying, that was no real reason to celebrate. Patrick Hohmann's parents reacted even more strongly. Gerhart Hohmann cut back his son's monthly study contributions. When Elisabeth Holdener and Patrick Hohmann were married in 1972, the Hohmanns only attended the church service and not the reception afterwards. "I was very hurt by this," explains Patrick Hohmann. However, his brothers Charles and Kevin joined in the celebrations, a gesture of support for which the newlyweds were extremely grateful.

The couple now had to rely on themselves. Elisabeth Hohmann Holdener moved to Reutlingen. She only needed to obtain a qualification in gymnastics to complete her teacher training, and she could do so later, when her son Patrick junior was six months old. Patrick Hohmann began a double life. He worked nights as a porter or did piecework ironing at a laundry: he loaded about 80 shirts per hour onto a metal mannequin to push them through the heated cabinet. In the daytime, he attended courses at the Technikum. But then he had a stroke of good luck. As part of a work internship, he found a job as permanent assistant to the production manager. The company Fallscheer had a spinning mill and dyeworks on the River Echaz. The company produced yarn from acrylic fibres. When the German textile industry gradually came under pressure, this had a knock-on effect on Fallscheer. Germany became too expensive as a location for the textile sector, as the profit margins were too tight. The cheap products from abroad made it tough for locally produced textiles.

The production manager appreciated Hohmann's hard work doing his rounds in the company wearing a blue coat with a pen and a slide rule in his breast pocket. When his manager realized that his sector had an uncertain future in Germany, he decided to emigrate to El Salvador. Maybe Patrick Hohmann would like to take over his job? "I didn't have any problems with the technical side," emphasizes Hohmann, who was still studying when he began the job in 1974. His role was to check the consistent quality of the yarns and to boost production by increasing machine speed. "But managing 120 people, including 60-year-old master craftsmen, was an entirely new experience for me as a 26-year-old. There were also problems with the salaries. My first task was to shut down the dyeworks, since the environmental agency insisted on this. The owner of the company was almost bankrupt. I tried to draw up new calculations for the yarn, but then I noticed that I was the only one who was interested at all in the calculation. I had asked my professor for help, until eventually he said, 'Forget it, it's hopeless.'" When Hohmann finally could no longer rely on the owner's word about paying the outstanding salaries, he decided to hand in his notice.

Meanwhile, word had got around that Hohmann was hard-working. BSU, a spinning mill near Hohmann's employer, heard that the Arabic-speaking textile engineer was looking for a new job. The company had just opened a subsidiary, BSU Trading & Consulting. The idea was, in partnership with major machine manufacturers and with European Economic Area (EEA) funds, to establish spinning mills that were closer to the growing regions. BSU would purchase yarns from the spinning mills and make extra profit from the resale. The producing countries in Arabic and South American regions could create more jobs. Thanks to the sale of the yarns back to BSU Trading & Consulting, they could also pay back the loans agreed by the EEA. The idea was tempting, but unfortunately theory and practice did not coincide. No yarn was supplied from the Arabic regions and there were delays with the loan payments.

Patrick Hohmann was sent to check what was wrong on site. He travelled to Sudan, back to his old home, where he discovered some eye-opening shortcomings. A spinning mill had been built in the desert, miles away from any electricity and water. Another plant had been offloaded on the desert floor that shifted, causing constant production stoppages and damage to the machine fleet. A third plant was finally operational, but then came to a standstill because of a lack of spare parts. In conversation with the locals he then discovered that more equipment was left standing in the desert, which would take several days to reach. Hohmann notified the Sudanese government and decided to set off looking for spare parts. He rented a jeep and drove with a small delegation hundreds of miles across the desert, cut off from communication with the outside world. The vehicle, the only one that could be rented in Khartoum, was not suitable for off-road travel. Now and then, everyone had to climb out and push the car, if possible, before nightfall and before the scorpions crawled out of their hiding places. "I can still remember it well," recounts Hohmann. "Alcohol was banned in Sudan, but somehow we had organized a bottle of date schnapps, which we passed round. We sat outside beneath the starry sky when I asked Mohammed

Saleh, 'How far is it from here to the Nile?' His answer was, 'At least 4 kilometres, if not more.'" This response was a light bulb moment for Patrick Hohmann. It had a long-lasting influence on him, motivating his lifetime wish for genuine intercultural exchange. "I asked myself, what is he actually saying to me? He's not saying, 'The Nile is really close.' I realized that his way of thinking was completely different to ours. What he meant was, 'The Nile is a short distance away.'"

During the expedition to the desert, not far from the pyramids at Meroe, they actually discovered the gigantic wooden crates with the coveted spare parts. Back in Khartoum, Hohmann applied to the Sudanese government for permission to transport the crates from Meroe to use the parts in the defective plant at Hajj Abd Allah. The government shrouded itself in silence; the authorization never came. Hohmann finally ordered the missing parts in Europe and managed to get one plant operational from three phantom plants.

Elisabeth Hohmann Holdener: Wife, Ally and Sparring Partner

"In fact, I just wanted to impress my wife and buy her a gift – a red Porsche."

Patrick Hohmann met 17-year-old Elisabeth Holdener at a dance school, which was appropriately named the "Eden", in Brunnen. It was Shrove Tuesday, 8 February 1969. Elisabeth Holdener was not so keen on dancing, but a friend persuaded her to join in. As for Patrick Hohmann, he rarely went out in the evenings. His parents preferred him not to go out partying with friends. This time, however, they turned a blind eye because the Hohmann family had a guest from New Zealand. Scott Rutherford, 19 years old, like Patrick, was visiting Aegeri for a few days. Hohmann's parents could not easily refuse a request from the grown-up son of their friends. So, the two young men set out together.

When Patrick Hohmann met Elisabeth Holdener it was the much-lauded love at first sight. Yet, it was Scott who danced with Elisabeth, while Patrick stood at the bar and watched them. The cool, laid back Scott finally managed to find out that the young woman had plans to go skiing at the weekend on the Stoos, the local mountain in Brunnen. If the weather was fine, they could also meet up there. Of course, why not?

On the day of the meeting Patrick Hohmann was so worked up that – deep in conversation with Elisabeth Holdener – he forgot the hard shells of his ski boots in the spa hotel on the Stoos and went to the ski station wearing only the soft inner liners. After the skiing excursion he would say to one of his best friends,

"At last, a girl that you can also talk to." The romance started less intensely for Elisabeth Holdener. They met up on their free afternoons at Lake Lucerne and talked for hours. From the outset, they were captivated by their mutual conversations. Officially, Patrick Hohmann was 'learning' French and English vocabulary. His teachers at the boarding school might have overlooked that their protégé hardly needed to learn vocabulary in his native French and English. "Things started out really well," recalls Elisabeth Hohmann. "And it was also fine like that."

Elisabeth and Patrick Hohmann have now been married for 50 years. "A blessing," remarks Patrick Hohmann. Good fortune alone doesn't last for such a long time. "I love my wife dearly, because she gave me a purpose in life and supported me on my journey," says Patrick Hohmann and laughs when he thinks of the aspiration he felt starting out his working life, or his desire in those days to earn lots of money. "In fact, I just wanted to impress my wife and buy her a gift – a red Porsche," explains Hohmann. "But Elisabeth wasn't at all interested in a Porsche."

What Elisabeth Hohmann dreamed of was certainly not speed, flashy cars and being a petrol head. She wanted to have children and would have liked to have six of them. After the birth of Patrick Jr, Elisabeth Jr, Simon and Martin, it became clear to her that she had her hands full with four children, especially since Patrick was often away during their childhood. Elisabeth Hohmann more or less brought up their four children single-handedly. She was the one who looked after the children, supporting their activities, coping with their difficulties at school and caring for the house, garden and pets. She drove the children to school and worried about each child on her own. The grown-up children now recount with great warmth and affection the time they spent with their mother. "Sometimes, my mother woke me very early in the morning

Top | **From left to right: Patrick Jr, Elisabeth Hohmann Holdener, Patrick Hohmann (back), Simon, Martin, Lisa (front).**

Top right | **Patrick Hohmann and his wife give the gift of a cow to a deserving farmer.**

Bottom right | **Elisabeth Hohmann Holdener always supported the organic cotton project, regardless of the ups and downs.**

MAIKAAL

and then we watched the sunrise together, just me and her. That was wonderful," enthuses the youngest son Martin Hohmann. Patrick Hohmann was absent for weeks and months at a time, and this was in an era when communication was restricted to very occasional telephone calls or a few dry lines in a telex message. "The occasions when Patrick was present," admits Elisabeth Hohmann Holdener, "were rather few and far between. If he was there, he came home from the office for lunch at midday. He explained what was happening with the dollar exchange rate, or that the company had sold two container loads of cotton. He hardly participated in the children's conversations, often not really knowing what they were talking about. But the children always sensed that he wanted the best for them." Patrick Hohmann was a strict father; clearly, he was influenced by the rigid, rather cold upbringing that he had experienced. The children enjoyed the holidays together all the more. Their father was relaxed then and had time for them. The family set off in the camper van with a tent in search of adventures away from the beaten tourist track.

The challenge in the Hohmanns' marriage was Patrick Hohmann's parents who bluntly rejected their daughter-in-law and maintained this attitude for decades. Ellen Hohmann Collins, in particular, was dissatisfied with her son's choice and let Elisabeth Hohmann Holdener feel that she wasn't the match that she had imagined for her son. The plain fact that her daughter-in-law was Swiss went against her. Ellen Hohmann Collins had little time for the egalitarian sides of Switzerland. After losing their businesses in Egypt and Sudan, the cosmopolitan woman arrived rather involuntarily in Aegeri, Canton Zug. From 1971 the family's focal point gradually shifted to this small village. Patrick Hohmann's parents owned a modest holiday house here; it had a wood fire and in the winter they were regularly snowed in. Ellen Hohmann Collins was accustomed to being surrounded by domestic servants. To find herself in the countryside again, cut off from the diversions of a big city must have felt like a social comedown for her, an excruciating exile in a dull region. She never learned Swiss German.

Patrick Hohmann's mother would have preferred her son to marry the daughter of a Parisian lawyer, or an English aristocrat, at least a woman from supposedly higher social circles. She had to be Catholic and have the social graces to circulate in polite society. Elisabeth Holdener didn't live up to these aspirations. She was from a loving, open parental home. Her father Armin Holdener was a salesman and took an interest in the arts. Elisabeth Holdener Amiet, her mother, was a housewife and spontaneously liked her future son-in-law. Patrick Hohmann also had a very good relationship with Elisabeth's mother and her sister and brother. "Patrick's parents were old school. They almost bowed, if a banker met them. I had a much more liberal upbringing. My grandmother divorced at a time when it stirred up gossip. My grandfather was interested in Rudolf Steiner, but he said he wouldn't tell the priest, otherwise he could still end up in hell. I wasn't interested in what people said or thought about me, or how they were dressed. Although his family was against me, Patrick supported me wonderfully," comments Elisabeth Hohmann.

The loyalty was mutual. Elisabeth Hohmann quickly noticed that Patrick had found his vocation in the textile industry, that he loved travel and was fascinated to learn about other cultures. She supported him unconditionally. When she was pregnant with her first child, she followed her husband to Reutlingen, a city, where she never felt at home. She had grown up on the shores of Lake Lucerne and was accustomed to open vistas across the water; she found little pleasure in Reutlingen.

"Sometimes, I had the feeling that I was dying of thirst," she says. When Patrick Hohmann failed his exams at the Technikum because his night shifts gradually took their toll, Elisabeth Hohmann accepted a job as a secretary to make ends meet for the small family. In Reutlingen, sometimes money was so tight that they stood on the balcony and longingly wondered whether there was enough money to share an ice cream down in the petrol station forecourt.

Patrick Hohmann could also count on his wife later. In 1979 when the Hohmanns returned to Switzerland, they were both in their late twenties, had four children and no money. The textile industry in Switzerland was in crisis. Patrick Hohmann applied for one of the rare jobs at the Heberlein company in Wattwil. He took the lift in the high-rise building, came back and sat with his wife in the car. "It smells strangely of carpet up there. I cannot do that," Patrick Hohmann admitted to his wife. His suggestion to her was to become self-employed; she agreed. "Financially, it was often difficult, but I always had great faith in Patrick," says Elisabeth Hohmann looking back.

The Hohmanns' marriage was only seriously under threat once in 50 years. The conflict flared up because Elisabeth Hohmann wanted to send her children to the Steiner school. 1983 was a terrible year: Patrick Hohmann had just filed for bankruptcy with his company Hohmann GmbH. He had no idea how he should afford the private school where Elisabeth Hohmann wanted to send her children. He was not only against it for financial reasons. During his childhood Patrick Hohmann endured the painful reality of repeatedly being uprooted. He definitely wanted to spare his children the same experience. His children should attend school where the family lived. They should remain part of the village community and not be isolated from their classmates in the neighbourhood. The Steiner school was in Baar which was further away. Hohmann worried that his children could lose contact with their friends in the village. Then there was his intuitive dislike of the mindset of Rudolf Steiner that he felt no affinity with.

Rudolf Steiner was born in 1861 in present-day Croatia; he died in 1925 in Switzerland, in Dornach near Basel. Steiner was the founder of anthroposophy, a philosophy of life, which involved very different spiritual and religious movements, for example, German Idealism in the Goethean sense, Christian mysticism, gnosis and oriental teachings. Steiner was an incredibly productive intellect, a prolific writer and a tireless lecturer. It was not uncommon for him to have three appointments in three different places on the same day; he often wrote his speeches on the way from one speaking venue to the next. He claimed to have received the countless insights, which he conveyed to his audience, in a moment of clairvoyance. To this day such aspects hardly make Rudolf Steiner's works easy reading, because the study of his texts relies not only on intellectual understanding. One must also read Steiner from the heart, and perhaps more with a spiritual, almost metaphysical sensibility. In devising anthroposophy, Steiner was essentially concerned with "an equally grandiose and occult 'cosmogony', which was a coalescence of all imaginable topics and areas of knowledge from cosmology to the natural sciences and cultural and religious history to a unique evolutionary history not only of humanity, but also of the earth and the entire cosmos."[3] The interesting factor about Steiner is that he had begun his intellectual career in mathematics and natural sciences. However, in 1891 he wrote his dissertation in philosophy with a study of the philosopher Johann Gottlieb Fichte. He developed this interest soon afterwards into his main work "The Philosophy of Freedom".

The enduring popularity of Steiner's teachings is due to the combination of science and spirituality, of empiricism and sentiment. Steiner always motivated his followers to critically support him and his ideas and to back up what actually emerged from these ideas with empirical evidence. This explains why primarily Steiner's practical incentives were integrated into the heart of society. The Waldorf system, or progressive education devised by Rudolf Steiner with its ethos of nurturing the child to be part of the community and to take self-responsibility became a long-established programme of alternative education. The same applies for biodynamic agriculture. Previously, it was regarded as a curiosity and treated with ridicule and astonishment, but organic farming and its Demeter products found their way onto the shelves of major distributors. It is seen as a sound answer to the lifeless mass production of agriculture.

"I introduced Patrick to anthroposophy, although originally he raised strong objections," Elisabeth Hohmann stood firm. She was unrelenting in her arguments for her children's education. "I forced through the Steiner school; I remained obstinate." Her personal memories of her school days were not good; she attended Catholic institutions, first the Theresianum in Ingenbohl, then the Institut Ste. Agnès in Fribourg. "I always asked questions, but Catholicism was so narrow-minded. I thought that answers must be out there." When Elisabeth Hohmann met the concert violinist Hilde Mlosch, who taught at the Steiner school in Baar, she began to take a serious interest in the Waldorf approach to education, "I closed the door on Catholicism. Patrick found it much more difficult to release himself from it." There were fierce disagreements. When Patrick Hohmann understood that his marriage was at stake, if he didn't give in, he finally announced that he was willing to send his children to the Waldorf school. However, he wanted to know what his children would learn there. “I will concentrate on reading up about Rudolf Steiner,” he promised his wife.

Patrick Hohmann kept his word. He quickly familiarized himself with the cosmos of Rudolf Steiner. And to his amazement, he was gripped by the ideas and the worldview of anthroposophy. Hohmann also got involved – as was expected of Steiner pupils’ parents – in the school administration. He took an interest in the finances of the Steiner school in Baar. On Tuesdays, together with his wife, he attended the “Zweig”, a group that read and discussed Steiner’s writings. The discussions often continued when Patrick and Elisabeth Hohmann arrived home. Over the years, Elisabeth Hohmann remained his most important conversation partner. “Elisabeth always persistently asks questions, and I prefer not to answer them. I need a lot of time to think through certain ideas. I don’t like discussing incoherent ideas, because they are fixed as soon as I mention them. Elisabeth’s demands of me are therefore very important,” explains Hohmann.

Patrick Hohmann owes a great deal to his wife’s persistence. Without her constant persuasion, he would probably never have found a way to spirituality and certainly not have studied Rudolf Steiner’s work. In turn, without immersing himself in the ideas of Rudolf Steiner, the textile and cotton dealer Patrick Hohmann would hardly have become convinced that one must basically reassess things and find new ways to tackle them. Although Hohmann joined a working group led by the anthroposophical economic reformer Udo Herrmannstorfer, he often felt alone with his thoughts here. “The members of the working group were mainly small businessmen, but also several would-be entrepreneurs,” Hohmann recalls. One day, he telephoned Udo Herrmannstorfer because he had a question. “His wife was on the phone. She said impatiently that we should finally leave her husband in peace and think for ourselves." Patrick Hohmann laughs, as he relates this. "I had never phoned Herrmannstorfer before then. But I thought: the woman is right. I must concentrate on my own ideas to develop what I really think."

A Cotton Dealer Goes Bankrupt

"I still see him today coming up the path to the house. Patrick was totally crestfallen."

In 1979 before the birth of Martin – the Hohmanns' fourth and last child – the family returned to Switzerland. Elisabeth Hohmann had looked for weeks for an apartment, now for their six-strong family, though to no avail. The Swiss landlords were stubborn; no one was willing to offer them a rental contract. Nothing could be done without a salary statement and proof of earnings from self-employment. Finally, the events of the day came to the Hohmanns' aid. In Meierskappel, a village on Lake Zug with 600 residents, Elisabeth Hohmann viewed a detached house whose sale had fallen through. The owner had planned to sell his property to a German. However, a Federal Council resolution, the so-called "Lex Furgler" ruling, had upset the plan. The Swiss parliament had passed this new legislation that was meant to prevent what was described as "the sell-off of home" by prohibiting real estate transactions with foreigners. The Hohmanns had no capital, but a second coincidence came to their rescue. The owner of the house knew Elisabeth Hohmann's father and suggested to the young couple that they could purchase the house under a rent-to-own arrangement. "This house was the basis for our entire later life," explains Patrick Hohmann.

The early period of self-employment included the good-years. Hohmann GmbH, which the young businessman ran from the ground floor of the house in Meierskappel, traded yarn from Sudan, Korea and Brazil. Hohmann sold 4000 tonnes of yarn per year. The company turnover was roughly CHF 40 million, making it a rather small player in the market. Hohmann had agreed with his former employer, BSU Trading & Consulting, that he was allowed to continue using the contacts to the suppliers and customers. BSU had given up commercial trading of the subsidiary BSU Trading & Consulting because cheap import yarns were slowly jeopardizing domestic business. It was a classic case of cannibalization, but if Hohmann wanted to try things on his own account, BSU had no objections. Hohmann, who was always curious and interested in innovations, had even set up a second, smaller company: Remei AG. The name comprises the initial letters of the word for accountancy 're-' ('Rechnungswesen') and 'mei' from Meierskappel. The company basically consisted of a large computer. Because its acquisition was not worthwhile just for Hohmann GmbH, the company sold its computing capacity to other local small businesses so they could complete their accounts.

Among Hohmann GmbH's customers was the former GDR that placed orders through a company in Vienna. Fürst Kraus & Co. was one of numerous procurement firms in the West that supplied East Germany with consumer goods. Patrick Hohmann's contact in Vienna was Wolfgang Mahrer, the managing director of Fürst Kraus & Co. A second major purchaser for the yarns from Hohmann GmbH was located in Greece and manufactured bed linen. Every month five transporter consignments of cotton yarn drove to Thessaloniki, each truck load was worth CHF 100 000. Hohmann's business made advance payments until the fitted sheets were manufactured from the cotton yarn. His local bank held bank guarantees against the Greek purchaser, so ensuring liquidity for Hohmann GmbH. Everything worked smoothly until 1983. Then suddenly Hohmann's bank suspended the loan. It transpired that the financial institution had not carried out due diligence. Instead of insisting on an actual bank guarantee, the bank had accepted a bill of exchange that had not been authenticated – as Hohmann presumed – by a Greek bank and was merely signed by the Greek factory owner. When the Greek partner stopped his payments, the knock-on effect was the cancellation of the loan for the yarn merchant from Meierskappel. Hohmann suddenly had a shortfall of three million in the cash account.

Shortly before Easter 1983 Patrick Hohmann drove to Thessaloniki. Here, he spoke with his business partner and tried to salvage what could be saved. In fact, he found seven loads of fitted sheets in the warehouse out of the total 30 consignments owed to him by the Greek partner. He suggested to his debtor that he would accept the goods as payment and as partial compensation for the accrued debts. His Greek business partner agreed. The lorry convoy got under way with its agreed destination of Switzerland, where Hohmann intended to find other buyers for the bed linen. Hohmann flew back to Switzerland and waited, however, the convoy never arrived. His business partner had betrayed him a second time. His Greek counterpart had diverted the trucks and sold their consignment. When Patrick Hohmann could finally react, the Greek factory owner had already filed for bankruptcy. That sealed the fate of Hohmann GmbH. Yet, Hohmann also filed for bankruptcy so that he could first reimburse his other suppliers. He went to the magistrate and deposited the balance. "I still see him today coming up the path to the house with slouching shoulders. He was totally crestfallen. I felt so sorry for Patrick," says Elisabeth Hohmann in retrospect.

The family now experienced hard times when they were living from hand to mouth. Their daughter, Elisabeth Seiler

Hohmann, remembers it, “Although the situation was extreme, as children we were doing fine. Dad’s BMW was collected and we didn’t really understand why. Of course, it was different for my mother.”

Patrick Hohmann’s parents-in-law Armin and Elisabeth Holdener were worried and sympathetic, especially since the rift deepened between the bankrupt businessman and his parents. In fact, Gerhart Hohmann, who had a lifelong dream of a seat on an executive board, was a member of the board of directors of Patrick Hohmann’s local bank. His father was not so inclined to assist his son by requesting an explanation from the bank about how it had managed to accept a worthless bill of exchange as a guarantee. Conversely, Patrick Hohmann felt inhibited from taking action against the bank whose executive board included his father.

What was there to do in this existentially challenging situation? “An entrepreneur finds solutions,” maintains Patrick Hohmann, whose remark sums up in a nutshell his perception of entrepreneurial raison d’être. The primary and paramount role of a businessman, in his view, is to develop ideas to deal with complex situations in a pragmatic way. In 1983 this meant that Hohmann had to start from scratch. Instead of purchasing goods on his own account and selling them on for profit, the yarn specialist worked as an agent. Hohmann had to do things in a more modest way, since he no longer obtained credit that was vital to trade and make advance payments on his own account. Henceforth, he acted as an agent who sells yarns from spinning mills to purchasers that produce fabrics from them. Besides, it turned out to be a happy coincidence that his ownership of Remei AG was unaffected by the bankruptcy of his other company. By now, his ex-boss from Reutlingen, Rolf Schneider, was working at Teamco in Geneva. Hohmann sourced and sold yarns via Remei AG for Teamco. His suppliers, which he had narrowly managed to pay, remained loyal to him.

On occasions, the procurement of yarns called upon Hohmann's business ingenuity. For example, based in Europe it was impossible to contact the Sudanese spinning mill in Hajj Abd Allah, which was in the middle of the desert – there was no telex or telephone. Patrick Hohmann solved the problem by arranging for two lorries to drive weekly from Hajj Abd Allah to Port Sudan, no matter whether they were full or empty. The shipping company at the port, which had a telex machine, notified the yarn dealer in Meierskappel every time about whether and when he could expect the merchandise and with what consignment.

In the 1980s the Sudan business imploded. The problems had already emerged in early 1980. In March of this year Patrick Hohmann was in Khartoum when five army officers attempted a coup to remove President Jafaar Muhammad an-Numeiri from power. Numeiri himself had come to power as the result of a coup back in 1969. Like Nasser, his Egyptian role model, an-Numeiri had carried out socialist and pan-Arabic reforms. Patrick Hohmann was marooned in his hotel room, while the fighting went on outside in the streets. "I could see the dead from my window. Then I did what my mother had taught me: I ripped up all my papers, every clue about my relationships and flushed it all down the toilet. I only kept my passport," recalls Hohmann. On 25 March 1980 when the airport was re-opened, he finally managed to leave the country. Even as a Swiss national he could not be sure how the rebels would treat him, all the more so due to his long-standing relationships. "I couldn't contact Elisabeth. Therefore, my colleagues, some of whom were from Munich, sent a telex to the Hotel Four Seasons in Munich with the request to let our wives know that we were alive. We knew that this hotel had to have a telex machine. The hotel really did phone Elisabeth. But I only found this out when I was back in Switzerland again." The officers who had instigated the coup were arrested, but riots broke out in Sudan, and in 1985 they culminated in the removal of the authoritarian head of state. As a result, Hohmann began to concentrate on the Central African market and made contact with spinning mills in Zambia and Tanzania. The spinning mills here had no market access, so Hohmann made them an offer to act as their agent. He accepted an agreed commission and negotiated the prices on their behalf and transferred the money to the spinning mills.

Patrick Hohmann was to become caught up one more time in the maelstrom of historical events. Like the West, the GDR had supplied developing countries with machines for the textile industry with the idea that these countries could pay off the plants by supplying East Germany with the yarns. When the yarns were supplied from India, but their quality was unsatisfactory, the Viennese procurement company Fürst Kraus & Co. was called in. Wolfgang Mahrer asked Patrick Hohmann to pay a visit to the Indian spinning mills to see how production of the yarns could be improved. As he had previously done in Sudan now Patrick Hohmann was travelling as an engineer for special commissions on the Indian subcontinent. "I drove for weeks at a time in a hire car from one spinning mill to the next, often I only arrived at the mills at 10 o'clock in the evening. I checked the goods and explained the 'corrective actions'. I invariably slept in the car because there were no guest rooms," the spinning mill technician relates.

In January 1990, three months after the fall of the Berlin Wall, 4000 tonnes of cotton yarn were on order for East Germany. To be on the safe side, Hohmann called Wolfgang Mahrer in Vienna. "Will you take delivery?" he asked Mahrer. "No," he admitted, so Hohmann recommended to the Indian business partners immediately to stop the supplies and to sell the consignment on the open market. Shortly afterwards, Mahrer and Hohmann drove to East Berlin to visit the GDR's foreign trade operation Textilkommerz. This would be recorded for posterity as the 'transition period' between the Cold War and German unification. At this time, nobody really knew how things would turn out. The East German customers no longer wanted to fulfil their contract. Hohmann and Mahrer negotiated with them for compensation and were finally allocated CHF 150 000. "We paid this money without deductions to the Indian spinning mills. Today, my lasting relationships with several Indian spinning mills date from this period, in some cases the third generation already manages the mills," explains Hohmann delightedly.

The bankruptcy in 1983 was a turning point in Patrick Hohmann's life and in his family's life. "It was a difficult time," as Hohmann admits himself. But how did Tony Rinaudo, the winner of the 2018 Alternative Nobel Prize, describe this? "If you're desperate, you're standing on holy ground." The bankruptcy made Hohmann more aware of human vulnerability and reinforced his belief in business activity as a cooperative process, where the focus on money is only part of the overall activity. "I admire my father for what he achieved," says his son Patrick Hohmann Jr, who is also a businessman and has established a watch brand. "To set up a company that supports a social and ecological philosophy, and still chalk up success: that is a great balancing act. My father has proved that you can work sustainably as an entrepreneur and yet still be profitable." Until the bankruptcy, Patrick Hohmann was favoured with success as a businessman. It is one of his strengths that he recovered from the bankruptcy with plenty of business improvisation to create a new professional identity. And he turned his personal weakness into deeply held holistic ideas about economic processes. “You need both things in life,” remarks Hohmann, “a bit of good luck and a bit of bad luck. Being human is all about experiencing the polarity.”

Patrick Hohmann and Jürg Peritz: Two Men Committed to Sustainability

---

"Patrick is an annoying perfectionist. I've learned a lot from him."

In 1993 Patrick Hohmann met the manager Jürg Peritz who hails from a family of musicians with Romanian roots. His father was a multitalented musician. Hugo Peritz, born in 1906 in Zurich, played the violin, saxophone, piano, clarinet and vibraphone. After arriving at first in New York during the Golden Twenties, Hugo Peritz settled in Zurich, where together with his brother, Bernhard, he founded a band called "Berry" that successfully toured throughout Switzerland. Bebop and Swing were the sounds that Jürg Peritz grew up with. The family accompanied the father's band on tour while Jürg and his brother, Peter, were of preschool age. The "Berrys" performed in front of international audiences, at the "Palace" in Gstaad, in Montreux at the "Casino" and at the "Esplanade" in Zurich. The band members – with Brillantine in their hair – wore stylish white jackets with black bow ties and after concerts they trudged through the snow in stylish plus fours. Jürg Peritz's mother, Edith Brunner, a beautiful lady who was always dressed in the latest fashion, began organizing the tours, arranging the performance venues, accommodation and looking after her two sons. In 1949 Hugo Peritz left the band of his own accord: he wanted to give his family a quieter life and took a permanent position with the radio orchestra at Radio Basel. The sons were to get a good education and later pursue 'proper' careers.

Patrick Hohmann and Jürg Peritz of Coop: two pioneers of organic cotton who together created a viable alternative for consumers.

From music to fashion

Jürg Peritz must have kept alive some of his family's wanderlust, since he realized early on that an office job in a bank or insurance company would not be right for him. Peritz was fascinated by fashion; he had inherited a flair for fashion from his mother, whom he liked accompanying as a child, whenever she went shopping. Peritz wanted to travel, to see the world and to be associated with people. After some time at Feldpausch and Jelmoli, he would make a meteoric rise at Coop, although he sees this more as a happy coincidence. Peritz is not one of the managers who planned out their career on the drawing board. "I have hired many people in my career," explains the former member of Coop's executive management. Until his retirement in 2012 Jürg Peritz was head of the marketing and procurement department and deputized for the CEO Hansueli Loosli. "Many people asked me how I made it to the top and what they had to do to progress. If I'm honest, I have to admit that most things cannot be planned. A lot depends on how you personally develop and whom you meet. Enjoying responsibility and being willing to work hard are also important prerequisites."

Coop: sustainability as a strategy

Jürg Peritz is an inconspicuous, wiry looking man in his early seventies; he has short grey hair and wears glasses. As soon as he begins to talk, he has an aura of clarity. Peritz always completes the statements, which he has begun, calmly and without undue hurry. He also has the ability to structure his ideas while delivering his comments, so you have the impression of being able to watch him think. Somehow, this seems like an adventure. Although the musician's son doesn't play an instrument himself, he is an avid listener of music, and possibly this influences the rhythm of his speech.

Jürg Peritz joined Coop in 1990 and in the beginning he was anything but happy here. This changed when Hansueli Loosli joined in 1992 and restructured the outdated cooperative structure to a dynamic corporate enterprise. The salesman and controlling expert, Loosli, not only put sustainability on the agenda, but he also established this as an integral part of the corporate mission and strategy. Jürg Peritz was happy with the pace and direction of the second-largest retailer in Switzerland. "I was lucky to come into an environment that suited me." As the purchasing manager for the food & non-food departments, he had the opportunity for many years to observe the pitfalls of global procurement. "I experienced Hong Kong when it was still a production location. The waste water from the dyeworks flowed straight into the river that often turned blue or red. The disastrous working conditions, which I saw on my travels, motivated me to look for solutions." When Coop launched the 'Naturaplan' label in the food sector and proceeded to consolidate it, Peritz thought more about how the insights from food production could be transferred to textiles. In reality, he was looking for a supplier of organic cotton. However, he couldn't find anybody, until one day he read about Patrick Hohmann in an article of the specialist trade magazine "Textilwirtschaft".

Not exactly enthusiastic

"I phoned Patrick Hohmann and already noticed on the telephone that Coop was not what he was imagining. Coop was big; Remei AG was small. I had to work hard to persuade him to meet me." The two men finally arranged to meet for a longer discussion in Egerkingen, at the "Kreuz" inn. Although Patrick Hohmann didn't doubt that Jürg Peritz took a serious interest in sustainability matters, he placed a big question mark over any potential cooperation. The retail trade giant, Coop, was well known for squeezing out small companies: this made Hohmann sceptical and cautious. Besides, it was uncertain whether Peritz would succeed in pushing through his idea within the company to offer consumers a sustainable alternative in the textiles sector. Setting up a partner cooperation with a large group like Coop also implied enormous risks for a small company like Remei AG. What if Coop decided to change its strategy? What if the sustainability strategy didn't pay for Coop in the longer term? What if Remei could not supply enough of the product because of a failed harvest? A change of personnel was also a cause of anxiety. Who could give a guarantee to Patrick Hohmann that Hansueli Loosli and Jürg Peritz would stay for long enough to establish a workable partnership with interested farmers?

Setting up complex infrastructure

It takes plenty of time, lots of patience and meticulous planning to produce organic cotton in large quantities. Three years alone are needed to convert from conventional farming of an agricultural plot to ecological farming methods. The farmers must be trained in field work as well as producing and using organic crop protection. The soil must recover from the pesticides that were used beforehand. And there are continual setbacks due to bad harvests, water shortages or farmers who make mistakes. Not least, enough experts must be available to carry out checks on the field and in the lab. Once these conditions are fulfilled, sowing can begin, which leads to the harvest half a year later. Then it takes another year for de-seeding, spinning, weaving or knitting, dyeing and finishing. This is a very long process that requires a buyer to make a conscious decision and to go along with this, if there is to be a real chance of change. Would Coop be prepared for this? "Come to India, then I will show you everything," Hohmann finally said to

Jürg Peritz, thinking that he could shake off the manager like this. But to Patrick Hohmann's amazement, Peritz did travel to India to see bioRe® India for himself. His comment was: "Everything made a good, reliable impression on me. You could to talk to those in charge. You could see how competent they were and how professionally everything was organized. The people were committed heart and soul to organic farming. Along with Patrick Hohmann's incredibly honest approach, this presented me with a convincing overall picture." A short, one-and-a-half page contract was drawn up that was the start of a unique commercial relationship for the Swiss retail trade.

A sluggish start

Starting out was not easy, even if the problems didn't exactly arise where they were expected. Although Jürg Peritz was not yet part of the senior management team at Coop, he was able to quickly convince them to offer its customers textiles made from organic cotton. A guaranteed purchase order also had to be agreed with Patrick Hohmann's Remei AG to set up a system for the longer term and to protect the farmers involved in the proj-ect. Coop's top management agreed to this. In return, Hohmann committed to an exclusivity deal: he would only supply bioRe® cotton in Switzerland to Coop. This allowed Coop to develop a unique selling point on the domestic market with bioRe® textiles. This was essential, because sustainability not only implied social and ecological responsibility. Peritz understood the idea of sustainability in a wider sense: the project also had to be future-proof with regard to commercial considerations as well as marketing. "Something only works out commercially, if it also has longevity. Sustainable products make little sense, if nobody buys them," says Peritz. It was helpful in this case to offer some-thing that especially Switzerland's second duopolist did not yet have in its product range. It also helped to establish Coop's position as an innovative first mover in the market for ecological textiles.

The rubber crumbles

However, in the early days, of all things, the weak point was the commercial viability. Jürg Peritz organized events and training courses from the outset to bring on board those involved in the sales team. But initially the sales assistants were hardly enthusiastic about the insipid-looking textiles that made their way onto the shelves. They found it difficult to sell them and it took a lot of dedication. The early collections launched in stores were undyed. The sustainable production criteria were so religiously adhered to that the products could no longer meet the usual general quality standards. There was a deluge of customer complaints and bad test reports. Quality problems with the T-shirts were a recurring theme. People struggled with twisted threads and fabrics that lost their shape. After the fifth wash, natural rubber disintegrated into little crumbs. This material was used instead of lycra to make the elastic straps in socks. But it annoyed the customers and lost a lot of good faith. "We started out as pioneers. We didn't have ten predecessors whose mistakes we might have learned from," Jürg Peritz describes the challenge. And he remembers the question that he often had to answer during these years, whenever he appeared before the senior management, "How long do you actually want to throw our money out of the window?" Today, Jürg Peritz knows the answer.

Remei AG before the partnership with Coop

The products made from organic cotton were a flop for three years. Peritz persisted: he even arranged for the entire management team to travel to India with Hansueli Loosli. The senior managers talked to the farmers and visited the fields. The visit fostered deeper understanding from Coop's management for the adverse conditions of growing cotton and for the unequal allocation of added value within the textile production chain. After this visit the Coop's directors stood four square behind Jürg Peritz and Patrick Hohmann. While Peritz continued to inform and motivate the sales staff, Hohmann looked for supplier factories that were prepared to commit to sustainability. After all, there was little sense in growing organic cotton, only to colour the cotton with dyes that were of dubious quality for health or polluted the environment. Suppliers with inhumane working conditions were just as questionable. Until he met Jürg Peritz, Patrick Hohmann was a yarn dealer who described the cultivation of organic cotton as his hobby. Remei AG, based in Rotkreuz, had set up ecological cotton farming in India and attempted to obtain market access on the international scene for the contract farmers and their products. However, Remei AG's main business at that time was not trading in cotton, but yarn sales, in particular, conventionally produced yarn and the first organic yarn for further processing for woven and knitted fabrics.

Nomadic industry

In 1993 and 1994 when the cooperation began with Coop, Patrick Hohmann entered new territory both in ecological and entrepreneurial terms. He consistently restructured his company so that garments could be created that could satisfy his sustainability standards for the entire creation process.

Basically, it was madness to stand alone against the forces of an industrial sector. Probably nobody in the industry would have wagered a single franc on Patrick Hohmann bucking the trend to develop an alternative business model, which was based on trust and reliability. The textile industry is a nomadic, globally operating sector that abruptly ends relationships, as soon as more favourable production conditions emerge elsewhere. The norm is the fragmentation of the production process and the allocation of individual work stages to countries that are located far apart. Price is the golden calf that everyone in the 'world of fashion' dances around or thinks that they have to dance around. Are Chinese seamstresses cheaper than those in Brazil? Then the fabrics are simply shipped from Brazil to China, and the clients move on. Local industries go into decline, the prices of local products are undercut to such an extent that they are no longer competitive. Is a country passing stricter environmental regulations? Then the industry completes the dyeing where the rules are not yet so restrictive.

Creating space for development

A strong motivation for Patrick Hohmann is proving possible what everybody else claims to be impossible. He did everything to create a real, mental and financial 'production space' where mutual cooperation and not conflict influenced the business relationships. He regarded his role as an entrepreneur as creating space for something new. "You have a million. But what for?" asks Patrick Hohmann. "Certainly not to hoard it or inherit it, but to integrate it into the productive cycle and mainly as an opportunity for something to evolve." Jürg Peritz and Patrick Hohmann wonderfully complemented each other to allow this 'something' to emerge.

From annoying perfectionist to textile expert

Jürg Peritz, who was a member of Coop senior management from 2006, quickly realized that organic textiles only had a chance on the market, if they could keep pace with the fashions and became part of a lifestyle trend. He looked for, and found, a stylist for Remei AG who could meet this ambition. Eliane Kobler became a key figure for the success of the Coop collections. Kobler had learned her craft by going back to the drawing board. After her apprenticeship as a dressmaker, she graduated from Zurich's School of Art and Design where she had taken the specialist course in fashion design. She then worked as a stylist for one of the most important fashion importers in Switzerland. Peritz had noticed her work in the modest Swiss fashion scene because of her strongly conceptual designs and her exceptional ability to create a 'look' for a brand and its fashion lines. Kobler, who had first-hand experience of the dire production conditions in the textile industry, was also more than happy to oversee the styling work for sustainably produced collections. Coop appointed Kobler to develop the Coop Naturaline, a range which successively incorporated textiles for women, men, children, babies and the home, for example, like towels, bed linen and tableware.

Patrick Hohmann had loyal partners in Julius Reubke and Alfred Egger at Coop who supported him in the bid, among others, to persuade the Basel chemical company CIBA to formulate dyes without the addition of heavy metals. At Coop, Egger was responsible for quality management in the non-food sector and monitored organic processes. On the other hand, Reubke understood exactly which toxins were contained in the dyes and how they had to be formulated, so that it was ultimately possible to drink the dyed water without any harmful effects. Moreover, it was a considerable challenge to produce lightfast dyes that did not fade after washing. After all, the sustainably produced garment should stay looking fresh for a long time.

Another of Patrick Hohmann's roles was to identify the managing directors of cotton ginning factories, spinning and dyeing mills, finishing plants and sewing factories, who were prepared to completely change their way of thinking and to embark on the long process of achieving the industry accredited SA8000 certification standard. SA8000 is a leading international norm that is intended to improve working conditions for employees. This involves maintaining standards on health and safety at work, working hours, fair remuneration and the right to be represented by and participate in consultations with a labour committee. To complement these initiatives in the producing countries, Remei AG opened a design department that created fashion made from organic cotton in cooperation with Coop's purchasing managers. Nowadays, Coop's Naturaline is regarded as a great success. Every year about 2 million items made from bioRe® cotton are sold in almost 2,500 Coop retail outlets in Switzerland.

"The textile industry is highly complex," remarks Jürg Peritz who has been involved with this industry throughout his professional career. "Patrick is a fascinating character. Well, he's an annoying perfectionist," admits Peritz with good humour. "Patrick worked his way up in an incredibly short time from an engineer specializing in spinning technology to a textile expert. He is never satisfied with an 80% solution; he carries on asking questions until things are perfect. I've learned a lot from him." Although both men respected each other and had a friendly relationship, they didn't always avoid conflicts. "Despite our friendship, I always maintained a certain distance because sometimes I also had to make tough decisions. For example, if I had to reject a delivery from Remei because it didn't satisfy the quality agreements, or if there were delivery delays," explains Peritz who retired from Coop's executive board in 2012.

Jürg Peritz has not stopped campaigning for sustainability and humane production conditionshe and Patrick Hohmann continue their joint commitment in the bioRe® Foundation whose president is called Jürg Peritz.

"Disenchantment really means: I deluded myself. I didn't look closely enough."

Indore, about 800 kilometres north-west of Mumbai, is a bustling town with small artisan studios, several factories and typical monoblock buildings with workshops for motorbikes and generators. In front of the clothes boutiques, colourful saris sway in the wind. Behind them, the new menswear is displayed on headless mannequins: slim-fit short-sleeved shirts and jeans with heavily faded legs. The kiosks selling homeware are flanked by bright green, bright blue and orange plastic cords. They are used decoratively to tie around the cows' necks. The city with two million inhabitants is regarded as India's cleanest city. In fact, the streets and gravel squares are swept clean. There is no rubbish anywhere, no carelessly discarded packaging and no PET bottles. The parks are manicured and look inviting.

Madhya Pradesh: fertile and impoverished

However, as soon as you leave the city the dense residential areas become less concentrated, and the views open out onto the diverse and picturesque countryside. Field upon field of crops stretch out and in the distance shrubs and the feathery leaves of the neem trees provide shade. The neem trees everywhere are typical vegetation for tropical and subtropical regions; they grow up to 15 or 20 metres tall. The tree bark, foliage and fruits are used for pharmaceutical products. Yellow-sprinkled mimosa trees line the side of the roads. You pass through villages with patched-up houses and crooked huts, overtaking ox carts and women bearing heavy loads on their heads. The children play with homemade toys or used car tyres. The lottery shop is usually the only colourful spot in the village. It promises hope, even if it is illusory. The soil is reddish or black; light soils are mixed with heavy clods of earth that is rich in clay. Gradually, from the undulating landscape, which is interspersed with flat plains, the terrain merges into the never-ending vastness of Madhya Pradesh. 72 million people live in this state in Central India, which is the heartland of Indian culture, and the home of the Hindi language. Most of the population in this state is impoverished, although the term 'poverty' is preferably avoided, since it always implies a gap which invites charitable generosity. Perhaps, it would be better to say that the people in Madhya Pradesh – they are overwhelmingly employed in agriculture – are incredibly industrious, hard-working and yet they can never get ahead. Madhya Pradesh also holds a sad record: the Central Indian state, which is predominantly agricultural, lags far behind in terms of economic development and ranks 26 out of 29 states in all. This is despite or perhaps precisely because Madhya Pradesh ranks as the third largest cotton producer, after Maharashtra and Gujarat States, on the Indian subcontinent.

Yes instead of no

On 2 August 1990 Iraq invaded Kuwait and started the second Gulf War with the violent incursion into the desert state. Patrick Hohmann will not forget the date so quickly, as this was the day when a man whom he had never seen before appeared at the Remei company headquarters in Rotkreuz. His name is Morgan Jalan and he is from a wealthy Indian family owning extensive tea plantations in northern India. Morgan Jalan's

ann
M.

an

father donated funds to invest in a cotton spinning mill. This mill was to be built in the Nimar Valley, 100 kilometres south of Indore, not far from a large river called the Narmada River.

Having heard of Hohmann and his abilities, Jalan hoped to persuade the Swiss spinning technology expert to become a partner and to benefit from his specialist expertise. Would he not join Maikaal Fibres Ltd.'s board of directors? Patrick Hohmann still clearly remembers the losses of his father's company in Egypt and Sudan. So he has a simple principle: no participation overseas. Jalan departed empty-handed, but he would not be Indian, if he didn't ask again soon afterwards. There are a billion people: with this much competition, you would get nowhere, if you didn't insist. Patrick Hohmann talked it over with his wife, and they both agreed: the answer remained 'no'. Purely to be polite, Patrick Hohmann met Morgan Jalan again for a drink in a bar in Mumbai. He explained to the Indian entrepreneur why he didn't want to join the board of directors of his spinning mill. As he left the bar, Jalan asked, "So, you're in?" Hohmann intended to refuse again, but to his amazement his answer was quite different. "Yes, I'm in." In retrospect, Patrick Hohmann remarks, "I don't know what it was. Perhaps it was a kind of blackout, or an impulse that was stronger than my conscience." Elisabeth Hohmann was not particularly pleased when she found out that her husband had agreed the opposite of what they had decided, however: "There are always things that are better left unsaid. It's just how it is. Patrick decided things and my opinion on them was: he should do that now, if he believes it is right. I sensed that it made him happy. He felt some strong urge to do this."

Organic cotton at the outset

The location was decided for the spinning mill. The discussions at the initial meetings of the board of directors in spring 1989 focused on which machines should be purchased and how the building should be structured. Naturally, the question also arose about where to source the cotton that they planned to spin. Morgan Jalan had in mind a dealer in Bhopal, a city located about 300 kilometres from the planned spinning mill. As they talked this over, however, Hohmann and Jalan realized that it was absurd to purchase the raw cotton in Bhopal, when cotton farmers were also located around the planned mill. The Nimar Valley is well protected, since it nestles between the mountains of the Vindhya Range in the north and the Satpura Range in the south. Fields in close enough proximity to the Narmada River could even be artificially irrigated. This was a significant advantage, as cotton plants need plenty of water. Hohmann and Jalan finally visited a nearby cotton farmer because they wanted to know more about local farming methods. What they found out from him was irritating and made the two businessmen think carefully. The farmer told them that while he earned one dollar per kilogram of cotton, he had already spent 70 cents on pesticides. Effectively, however, the pesticides cost twice as much, since the Indian state had a 50% stake in them. The real costs for the pesticides alone were now USD 1.40, i.e. far in excess of the market price, not to mention the farmer's salary.

This was the background for Patrick Hohmann's and Morgan Jalan's initial idea of cultivating organic cotton. Jalan's family already had experience growing organic tea and this was extremely positive. Why should they not also try organic cotton to improve the farmers' income?

Hohmann discussed everything with his then business partner Peter Tschannen. They devised the plan to cultivate organic cotton in the vicinity of the newly established Maikaal Fibres Ltd. Morgan Jalan's family, friends in Mumbai whom Hohmann talked to and also government representatives in

Tanzania all said the same thing: forget it! Organic cotton, what was that about then? Wasn't it just an absurd idea? Almost a year passed. However, when Morgan Jalan, Patrick and Elisabeth Hohmann were invited to an Indian wedding they seriously discussed the proposal again. Finally in 1991 Morgan Jalan, Patrick Hohmann and Peter Tschannen plunged into the adventure of organic cotton. They enlisted the support of a specialist in biodynamic and ecological agriculture, Tadeu Caldas, from Emerson College in Britain. To begin with, only a handful of organic farmers were involved over a relatively small area of 60,000 square metres. Patrick Hohmann had no experience of ecological farming. His main incentive was the realization that the farmers hardly scratched out a living and that organic cotton would perhaps change this. If European consumers were willing to dig deeper into their pockets for sustainably produced food, then they would certainly also be willing to pay in a similar way for sustainable agriculture.

Premium payments in arrears

At the outset, Patrick Hohmann had already promised the organic farmers a premium on top of the market price for their hard work in biodynamic farming. This worked well for several years. The farmers completed the three-year conversion process from conventional agriculture to farming organic cotton. Thereafter, they supplied the cotton and were rewarded with the market price plus the premium from Maikaal Fibres Ltd. At least, Patrick Hohmann thought that this was the case, until one day he made a nasty discovery while talking to the farmers: they had not received their premium. Maikaal Fibres Ltd. was two years behind with the payments. Morgan Jalan's assets were illiquid; the company Maikaal Fibres Ltd. was bankrupt and the money had not reached the farmers. Morgan

Jalan and Patrick Hohmann took a joint decision to reassign the responsibilities: Jalan would concentrate on the spinning mill, while Hohmann assumed responsibility for the farmers to whom he paid the overdue premiums out of his own pocket. He stepped down from his role on the board of directors and left the spinning mill to found bioRe® India in 2003. When he was asked about these unpleasant events, Patrick Hohmann remarked, "Disenchantment really means: I deluded myself. I didn't look closely enough. For outsiders, such things are often worse than for me. I simply look forwards." And as a further thought, "Incidentally, there are also cheats in Europe."

bioRe® India

The company bioRe® India is still located in the Nimar Valley today. Its headquarters are in Kasrawad, not far from the bankrupt spinning mill. The company premises has a handful of attractive brick pavilions with shade-giving verandas. The garden with lawned areas, vegetable beds, yellow and orange marigolds and paths lined with trees is peaceful and large enough to accommodate the farmers for training courses as well as many interested guests from around the world who are warmly welcomed here. A small sculpture stands in one of the pavilions and is decorated with flowers. It represents a Nandi bull, the animal ridden by the Hindu god Shiva. Right behind it, Patrick Hohmann has fixed a plaque with a quotation from Rudolf Steiner: "A healthy social life is found only when, in the mirror of each soul, the whole community finds its reflection, and when, in the whole community, the virtue of each one is living." This meaningful statement that refers to the nuances of an intrinsic relationship between the individual and the community is the cornerstone of bioRe® India Ltd. and the affiliated foundation bioRe® Association. In other words, the interplay between bioRe® Ltd. and the Indian bioRe® Foundation creates the kind of balance that is suggested by the phrase and that is so important for Patrick Hohmann.

CEO Vivek Rawal

Vivek Rawal (born 1979) is at the helm of the company bioRe® India. Rawal is the chief executive and full-time director, while Patrick Hohmann supports him as president of the board of directors. The other members of the management board are Indian experts – one of them is the human rights activist Rajagopal P.V., while two positions on the board are reserved for cotton farmers to ensure that the practical side is always represented. Rawal, who is bubbling with energy, has an unusual professional background. He hails from this region and is a biology graduate. He then tried for a position in the highly respected State Administrative Service. To receive a work contract in this field, you have to complete one of the world's most difficult examinations: only about 450 candidates are recruited from the annual 200 000 applicants. Rawal, who calculated his chances with biology were poor, also graduated in law studies where there were fewer applicants.

The exams for the State Administrative Service are in three stages. Candidates must be at least aged 21 to enter the service, although they are allowed to take the preliminary examinations earlier. Rawal completed the first round of examinations aged 19, and he passed. However, between the first and second stage of the exam something happened that he had not expected: the state excluded members of the highest Brahmin caste from employment "for an indefinite period". And Rawal was a Brahmin. It is important to remember that since independence the Indian state has gone to great lengths to ensure that all castes, in particular, those who are casteless or members of the indigenous population, so-called Adivasi, have adequate representation in the civil service and university study places. This subject is a recurring theme in political debates. Facebook is full of comments made by frustrated members of the 'better' castes. However, Rawal reacted pragmatically to the entrance restriction and the cul-de-sac that he was now in. He decided to switch to the private sector and registered for a postgraduate degree in social work. He worked for several years after his graduation for non-profit organizations in north India and in Delhi, including being in charge of youth employment at the SOS Children's Village.

However, Rawal was drawn back to his home region, although he was unable to find work in the Nimar Valley. So he decided to set up his own foundation for youth work. While he was looking for entrepreneurs who were willing to donate funds to the foundation, he met Ritu Baruah and Patrick Hohmann. They were impressed by Rawal's proposal and asked him whether he wouldn't prefer to realize the planned projects with the bioRe® Association. Rawal agreed. 2005 was an exceptionally happy year for the Indian expert, since he not only returned to his home, but he also got married.

A proper functioning community

A great deal has happened since then. The foundation bioRe® Association has substantiated the ambition to create strong communities and to act as a dialogue partner to find solutions for what the farmers regard as the most pressing problems. In allocating the foundation's funds, Patrick Hohmann emphasizes continuity, especially when difficulties arise and not everything runs smoothly from the start. Loyalty and the constant willingness to listen, to work on the relationship and solve problems collectively are of central importance for Hohmann. He jokes, "Everyone can give a gift and run away as well." The farmers can submit applications and participate in the projects to the best of their abilities. The “animation schools” were one of the first projects that Patrick Hohmann and Vivek Rawal tackled. This project was at the request of the organic farmers who had suffered for years due to the Indian state’s guarantee of the right to education for every child, although in practice the schools were so far away that children in sparsely populated areas had no chance of getting there on foot. Especially not in the monsoon season, when all pedestrian routes are flooded and the ground is so swampy that you make no progress. The schools were and are funded by Coop and other organizations. This is a gift with marvellous development prospects.

Presently, about 1200 children attend the bioRe® schools, which incidentally accept all children in the remote regions, not only the children of bioRe® farmers. In November 2018 the first young adults could receive their graduation diplomas at a special ceremony. However, the bioRe® secondary schools not only concentrate on academic diplomas, but also offer training in the skilled trades, for example, sewing, motorbike mechanics, basic electrical skills as well as computer training. All the courses are open to boys and girls and a glance in the workshops reveals a good mix of pupils. Lessons are bilingual in Hindi and English. The joint commitment has paid off and has been bearing fruit for many years. The schools could not have been set up without the farmers’ contribution. They made available buildings to set up a classroom for the youngsters, and they did most of the hard work constructing the schools.

Other projects include an independent company for handwoven organic fabrics, sewing studios where, for instance, school uniforms are made and – very importantly – a mobile hospital. This is also funded by Coop and visits remote places on certain designated days. First-class medical services are available on board: X-ray, ECG, a lab for blood tests, ultrasound and so forth. In addition to the immediate treatment, the mobile doctors also offer the invaluable service of correctly referring patients, if they need further treatment in a hospital. The roads in Madhya Pradesh are long and arduous, plus mobility is expensive for people who earn low wages. Travel to the wrong place can be fatal.

The business model

bioRe® India Ltd.'s actual commercial activity, that is, the cultivation and marketing of GMO-free organic cotton, is faced with huge challenges. Currently, bioRe® India Ltd. has individual contracts with 3,550 farmers in the Nimar Valley region. These farmers receive a purchase guarantee for 80% of their harvests. There is an additional premium of 15% for their efforts in organic farming. The premium is based on the average market price for cotton over the past five years.

Why is it important to offer a purchase guarantee? We already mentioned that risk is spread disproportionately in the global cotton trade. The weakest market participants bear the highest risk and, if they have to fund the cash shortfalls, they also pay the highest interest rates. "Actually, it should be exactly the other way around," comments Patrick Hohmann. "In the rich countries, where people can afford it, interest rates should be high and they should be low in the poor countries. In India, a 14% interest rate is normal."

Indian farmers get into debt when they buy the seed. Until the sale of their harvest they are more or less insolvent. Basically, they make a bet: they invest in the seed and hope that when they sell the cotton they will earn more than they have spent. However, this bet doesn't always work. The weather or pests can spoil their harvest. The farmers can also be left with their harvest because of global overproduction. The purchase guarantee gives an assurance of a minimum income for the farmers and it offers them a stake in the world market. "I don't want to create an artificial market," comments Hohmann. The purchase guarantee also rewards the individual farmer for his efforts: those who supply good quality obtain a better price. Those who supply bad quality receive the usual market price for this category. Patrick Hohmann is rather critical of a minimum price, which some fair trade organizations pay, because it does not account sufficiently for the individual's hard work. In any case, the purchase guarantee shifts the risk from the farmers to bioRe® India Ltd. and Remei AG in Rotkreuz. Remei AG maintains warehouses where the surplus cotton can be stored until the sales conditions improve. Alternatively, the company can sell off the organic cotton in the conventional market. This involves risks that cannot be underestimated for the company, because conventional market sales, in particular, do not cover the costs incurred with organic cultivation. Selling organic cotton for the price of conventional cotton is a purely loss-minimizing business.

The big organic cotton swindle?

Until 2010 bioRe® India was making good progress. Organic cotton was booming and about 7,000 farmers were contracted suppliers. At the bioRe® Training Centre in Kasrawad and in the villages the farmers were trained in biodynamic farming methods and taught a holistic perception of humans, animals and plants. Then came the shock: the daily newspaper "taz Berlin" published an article on 22 January 2010 with the headline, "The big organic cotton swindle?" The report claimed that organic cotton was also contaminated with genetically modified cotton. Patrick Hohmann felt secure because he knew the farming method, he knew the field monitoring tests and he trusted his employees. He also knew the tests in the lab where bioRe® India systematically monitored the cotton. Nevertheless, he arranged for thorough checks to be conducted for his entire yarn warehouse. One week later Marion Röttges, who was then still the manager of the Internal Control System (ICS), came into his office.

"You won't be spared anything," she said.

"What do you mean?"

"I commissioned a European lab to check our warehouse. Our cotton is also contaminated," Röttges informed him.

Genetically modified cotton or when facts create facts

In 1997 the first field trials were started in India with GMO cotton – this stands for 'genetically modified organism'. In India, the common expression is 'BT', which stands for Bacillus Thuringiensis, i.e. the protein that is part of the cotton plant and produces a toxin. In other words, a gene sequence is inserted which allows the plant to produce the BT protein. The idea behind BT-cotton was to modify the gene of each individual cell of the cotton plant so that the feared invasive pest (the pink bollworm) perishes as soon as it starts to eat the plant. The industry hoped for a plant that would make the use of pesticides redundant. Pesticides tend to distribute unevenly when sprayed onto the plant. This drawback was to be avoided by inserting the said protein. No matter where the pest tried to eat the plant, it would be killed. The industry also promised bigger harvests and better quality. For cotton, this means bigger fibre bolls that are easier to pick and with longer fibres. The regulators conducted a controlled trial to check what the industry promises were all about and whether GMO cotton could be permitted in good conscience in India. However, in 2001 the Indian state discovered that thousands of hectares of cotton had already been illegally cultivated with genetically modified cotton. The new technology was already in the eco system. Instead of starting criminal proceedings, the Genetic Engineering Approval Committee (GEAC) decided to take the bull by the horns. In March 2002 India approved the cultivation of GMO cotton. After China, India is the world's second largest cotton supplier.

Needle in a haystack

What had happened? Why was the bioRe® cotton genetically contaminated? Were all the fields contaminated or only some of them? Had the monsoon floods polluted the soil? Had pollen floated across from neighbouring fields where GMO cotton was being grown? So many questions; the search for answers was difficult. It turned out that the ELISA test method, which the Indian employees of bioRe® were using, only gave reliable results if the plant had already formed the proteins. The method was unusable as a pre-delivery check for seeds. The Bremerhaven-based lab Impetus Bioscience had adopted a different method to test the seeds known as Polymerase Chain Reaction (PCR), an innovative DNA analysis. The result was clear: the seeds that bioRe® had purchased from external seed producers were contaminated with GMO seeds. It was rather reassuring to realize that the wrong test method had been used. That could be changed. However, the implication of this result gave cause for alarm: in India, from now on it was clear that no seeds could be obtained that were reliably non-GMO. This insight was the start of major problems growing organic cotton in India, and till today it means large volumes of the Nimar Valley harvests must be earmarked for loss-making sales in the conventional trade.

Any cotton dealer other than Patrick Hohmann might have perhaps given up and relocated the business to a different country. But Hohmann stayed loyal to his farmers, despite the difficulties, and started to tackle the problem from a different angle.

Aggressive marketing

India, this continent of misery and wonder, welcomes novelty with curiosity and euphoria, which is difficult to imagine in industrialized countries. In India, the future is full of promises. It is a paradise, and getting here is perfectly possible, if you only embrace the new firmly enough. This unique quality has made India a major power in information technology. However, it also helped GMO cotton to make its breakthrough. The industry advertised the new, genetically modified seeds to local people with aggressive marketing techniques. Syngenta, Monsanto and other companies toured the villages with trucks and loudspeakers mounted on the roofs. Colourful posters were put up; there were entertainment programmes for the farmers, advertising films and small ads. The seeds had rather Bollywood-sounding names or evoked the world's powerful personalities. One variety called "Obana" was particularly popular; it was deliberately reminiscent of the American President whose powerful aura supposedly applied for the cotton seed as well.

At first, it all sounded promising. And at first, it also looked like the promises would come true. In fact, in the initial two to three years the use of pesticides declined. However, then the cotton bollworm developed resistance and the farmers, who had just been delighted that they could stop using the pesticides, had to look on helplessly as their harvest was destroyed by the cotton pest. This caused the farmers to use pesticides again. They were mainly battling the secondary pests, like white fly, that used the empty nests of the pink bollworm and became the primary pest. The industry went a step further and launched another genetically modified type on the market – BT II-cotton with two inserted proteins. This was unsuccessful: more insecticides are used than ever today; in comparison with 2006 double the amount of insecticides are in use.

Fifteen years after the widespread introduction of GMO cotton things were in a sorry state. The cases of people in BT cultivation areas becoming ill with cancer were significantly higher. They complained about breathing difficulties and skin rashes. There were many more suicides because the farmers incurred debts due to expensive seed purchases and because the costs for seed and pesticides sky-rocketed. Biodiversity declined; the bees were dying off and pests became more aggressive. Not only the pests, but also the useful insects were badly affected by the toxins. The "Coalition for a GM-free India" has calculated that the soil contains about 100 million kilograms of toxins because the BT-plants emit these substances through the roots into the ground. However, one can only speculate about the health of the soil. We only know of a tiny fraction, i.e. about 20%, of the beneficial microorganisms in the soil. As for the rest, this is terra incognita, which of course makes scientific comparison difficult. Field trials clearly demonstrated that the soil on the fields with GMO crops is quite different from the soil where GMO-free cotton is planted. However, it cannot be measured. You notice that the soil is looser and contains more and different types of worms, but no reliable statements can be made about the precise cause. The worst thing about GMO farming is that GMO-free seeds are no longer available in sufficient quantities. Almost every seed delivery, which should be non-GMO, also contains GMO seeds. Besides, most of the old, indigenous desi[4]-cotton varieties, which were extremely long-lasting and required little water, have almost completely vanished.

GMO dominance makes life difficult for organic farmers

Meanwhile, 70% of the Indian bioRe® harvest is sold to the conventional market because it is non-compliant with the strict standards that bioRe® sets itself. "We have no choice," says Vivek Rawal. However, he adds, "But we'll find one." Since 2007 and even more so since 2011 bioRe® has stepped up its role in the research and comparison of cultivation methods. In cooperation with the Swiss Research Institute of Organic Agriculture (FiBL) in Frick, bioRe® is conducting extensive field trials to compile cross-comparative data about conventional, biodynamic, organic and genetically modified cultivation methods. The aim is to obtain definite insights into individual growing methods, so that the facts, for example, might confirm the effects that the adopted methods have on the soil condition. However, the overarching aim is to be able to breed the GMO-free seeds in sufficient quantities and also a seed that promises good, bountiful harvests for this. bioRe® India has separate research trials on breeding and evaluation of non-GM cotton seeds under organic conditions. One trial was set up with the University of Agricultural Science, Dharwad, under the leadership of Dr. S.S. Patil, a leading cotton breeder.

Namaskaar gold: organic cotton has a future again

Beneath a finely stretched, large net tent the entire precious crop of a ten-year project grows in lush green rows. Thanks to painstaking efforts working together with the Indian university, bioRe® India has successfully cultivated and developed an old desi-type cotton variety. Namaskaar Gold, literally "Good Evening, Gold!", will exist as a variety and hybrid cotton.

So, what are hybrids? The environmental scientist Markus Kunz, who is responsible for supply management at Remei AG, explains it with the example of the donkey and horse. For instance, you cross the female donkey with the male horse and the offspring is an animal that demonstrates the best features of the donkey and the horse. As tenacious as a donkey and as powerful as a horse. Hybrids are not capable of reproduction in animals or plants. The seed industry has exploited this, in particular, by intensive advertising to launch the hybrids on the market, because the lack of reproductive ability amounts to an intrinsic protection of the varieties. The only cotton hybrids that so far exist in India are genetically modified. You have to imagine planting so that a row of mother plants and a row of father plants are grown alternately next to each other. Pollination is done by hand, an impressive and time-consuming procedure that was amazingly successful for the cotton farmers, because the seed capsules with the ripening cotton fibres inside grow especially large and yield correspondingly big white fibre bolls. bioRe® India has succeeded in breeding the first GMO-free hybrids on the Indian continent that produce comparable results in organic farming to the genetically modified method. These kinds of successes in 2018 earned state recognition for the Indian bioRe® research as an independent, organic research institute. Thanks to the research results, Patrick Hohmann is convinced that the soil can become healthy and biodiversity can be restored again. He prefers not to think about the sums that he has invested in research during recent years. Every year he had to account to the board of directors for six-figure investments without any obvious profit. “I was frequently asked: how long will it still take?” he relates and adds, “It takes a long time, a very long time. Ten to twelve years.” In 2019 or 2020 our own GM-free cotton seeds will be available in sufficient quantities as seeds for the bioRe® farmers. It is a research breakthrough for GMO-free seed. Perhaps, it is also a new beginning after the nightmare that has also affected other growing regions in India.

bioRe® Tanzania Ltd.

"I always maintain my distance, from royalty the same as from farmers."

Mwanza airport is small and easy to get around. The beige tower situated on a hill is surrounded by tropical vegetation. The reception building made of cement is flat and unassuming. You don't need to look for long to identify the people who are here to collect you. Outside in the car park, on the red compacted soil, a white four-wheel drive vehicle awaits visitors from Switzerland. The suitcases are quickly loaded and the vehicle sets off. Patrick Hohmann leans forwards and casts a worried gaze at the sky through the windscreen. The tropical sky is grey and overcast with big puffy clouds. "No rain today," says Niranjan Pattni, the managing director of bioRe® Tanzania Ltd. "I'm not so sure," replies Hohmann. If only it does not rain on the cotton, which is thick and fluffy in the opened fruit capsules, and is ripe for harvest. "No rain today," Pattni repeats and smiles. He will be right: no rain today, and no rain either tomorrow or on following the days.

It is a long journey from Mwanza on Lake Victoria to the Meatu District and the road is quite hazardous: the tarmac stops after a hundred kilometres and it is good advice to take care on the dirt track that continues in a south-easterly direction into the cotton-growing regions. There is not much traffic; most of the locals get about on foot, or they cycle from one village to the next by the side of the track and on ground that is overgrown with weeds. Ox carts appear, and young women pushing their water buckets home on handcarts. There is an electricity cable, which follows the road, but only a few houses are connected to it. Now and then a dust trail is visible in the distance. Then it is obvious: a cotton transporter is soon heading this way – the massive bright blue trucks approach us; they are piled tower-high with tightly packed, white sacks. In other words, forty tonnes are travelling at high speed and will not get out of the way. The slightest deviation can cause the trucks to tip over on the camber of the dirt track, causing accidents that often end in fatalities. It is vital to avoid this, and better to drive slowly to one side and give way, until the loud horn of the truck drones and fades into the distance.

The area south of Lake Victoria is flat as far as the horizon and its beauty is majestic and sublime. Large groups of baobab trees rush past, every one of the trees has a unique character; they can live for up to 800 years. Probably, elephants once lived here because baobab tree seeds lie dormant for some time and are 'awakened' as the animals digest the seeds. They can then grow into these imposing baobabs. Most of the cotton fields have already been harvested; the empty stalks are left to be stripped and chaffed. Now the farmers plant maize or millet whose beautiful umbels are silhouetted against the horizon like filigree cut-outs. The handful of cotton fields that are still ripening are dotted with pale yellow and pink-coloured flowers. Outside the fields grow black locust plants, sisal and chalky thorn bushes. Neem trees, which typically grow in tropical and subtropical regions, appear everywhere because they can tolerate the arid conditions. The farmers make a brew from their leaves that spoils the appetite of the cotton pest, the pink bollworm. Rows of sunflowers planted between the cotton also help to ward off the pests: they attract the harmful insects, while the surrounding cotton can continue to grow without any trouble. All around are large herds of cattle and goats, which are controlled by youths with sticks or by throwing stones. In Meatu, as in many of Africa's rural regions, the people very rarely keep a bank account. The bank account is four-legged – the cattle herds are a well-guarded treasure. The animals are sold as soon as ready money is available. If a farmer needs more cash, he goes to market and sells one of the animals.

Patrick Hohmann's relations with Tanzania go as far back as 1986. At that time he was purchasing cotton yarn from a spinning mill in Tanga, the country's northernmost port city. The CIC Textile Mill belonged to Chhotubhai Somaia, a convivial businessman who threw parties when Hohmann arrived; his home was a place for philosophizing, discussing and drinking plenty of whiskey until daybreak. Somaia's right-hand man was called Niranjan Pattni and Chhotubhai trusted him like his own son. The Tanzanian of Indian descent had studied chemistry, as well as working for a soap factory and eventually ending up via the clothing wholesale business in the textile industry. In 1994 Chhotubhai's son Yogesh started to grow organic cotton in Meatu. The district lies in the heart of the country, about 600 kilometres from Tanga. This region is especially suitable for cultivating cotton because of the arid conditions. Patrick Hohmann supported the project, but somehow things made little progress. The CIC Textile Mill suffered the same fate as so many factories in regions with weak infrastructure: it went bankrupt due to continual power failures.

Patrick Hohmann decided to take responsibility for the farmers and work with them directly. With Niranjan Pattni's support he founded bioRe® Tanzania, even though he had never once been in Meatu. When he travelled there with his business partner, he discovered an antiquated world which was

P. 102f. | **Training session to cultivate tomatoes in crop rotation, from l. to r.: Ndamo Basanda, Sawa Lugulu, Faustin Magalata, Esther Luhende, Masonga Luhende, Mahega Luchagula.**

Top | **from l. to r.: Niranjan Pattni (CEO bioRe® Tanzania Ltd.) in conversation with his team. Edward Gafungilo (Field Extensionist), Masanja Pambe (Field Extensionist), Faustin Magalata (Training Officer), Peter Kwilasa (Supervisor, currently: Production Manager), Alfred Sayi (Field Extensionist).**

Top right | **from l. to r.: Agnes John, Dorica Mhandi, Modesta Kwilasa at a cookery demonstration in Mwambegwa with an efficient cooking stove that saves firewood and offsets CO_2. Every farmhouse in the region has a separate cook house.**

Bottom right | **The most hard-working people – compared with those employed at the end of the supply chain-receive the lowest wages. bioRe® takes the pressure off the farmers thanks to a purchase guarantee and a premium for organic cotton. In the photo, Kabula Jiliala Lukomanga picks cotton. Her father and her uncle are contract farmers for bioRe® Tanzania Ltd.**

lacking in comfort. There was no electricity, no telephone and no accommodation, although there was plenty of sunshine and dust as well as the disappointed farmers who told them that they had never received the promised premium for their organic cotton. When Hohmann and Pattni travelled back to Meatu soon after, they packed money into a suitcase to pay the farmers the premium that they were owed cash-in-hand.

Patrick Hohmann and Niranjan Pattni have been friends since this day. Pattni has a rare gift: a sense of humour tempered by wisdom. When he talks about the achievements of the people in Meatu, about their misfortunes, successes and their craftiness, too, he laughs. However, his laughter is never gloating or hurtful. His laughter is forgiving, as though he were also laughing about himself or about this curious species humankind in general. Pattni is not one for giving orders. He is an excellent listener; he appears open and inspires confidence. This draws people to him; they like approaching him to ask for advice. Patrick Hohmann owes Niranjan Pattni a great deal, because without him it would have been very difficult to develop the growing area for organic cotton in Meatu. Initially, Pattni supervised the farmers from Tanga. In 2001 he moved full time to Meatu. This was a very challenging phase for him. He was separated from his wife, Priscilla, and his four children, who remained in Tanga, and each time he had to travel 160 kilometres to the capital Shinyanga to be able to call his family or to send them an email.

The accommodation in a rural guesthouse was modest like the owner's cooking skills. Insipid stewing chicken and bland, overcooked maize are still favourites in this region today. Whenever Pattni drove back to Tanga, he returned to Meatu with lots of dried food. It was not until bioRe® Tanzania moved its headquarters to Meatu in 2005 and built a group of buildings that things became easier for him. After the children had left home, finally in 2009 his wife Priscilla came to Meatu. She took over the secretariat at the headquarters of the ever-growing company; she helped to introduce smoke-free stoves and above all she took charge of the kitchen, which was an invaluable culinary asset for the whole area and for all the visitors to Meatu. "Priscilla has an incredible amount of energy," comments Pattni. "She has no problems working 14 hours a day."

The headquarters of bioRe® Tanzania is in Mwamishali (Meatu District), about 280 kilometres south-east of Mwanza. The centre incorporates a demonstration farm and offers the farmers accommodation when they attend the training courses. Some of them arrive on their own motorbikes. However, most of them are collected by bioRe® Tanzania with a bus, since they live a long way from the bioRe® centre, some of them as far away as 50 or 60 kilometres. The buildings are grouped around a central courtyard with flowering bougainvilleas. The bricks for the buildings were produced and fired locally. They had to be moistened with water and dried in the sunshine for many weeks to ensure that no cracks appeared. The site is protected by a barrier towards the street, however, there is no fencing. "I don't like fences," says Patrick Hohmann who was urgently advised by the local authorities to provide security for the site. Hohmann, who regards it as important that the head office is inviting and welcoming, pretended not to hear. And rightly so, because only a single break-in was reported in 13 years, and the culprit – an employee – was quickly caught. The site also has a friendly atmosphere because it is surrounded by several hundred neem trees. Before they depart, every visitor is invited to plant a tree and to fix a plaque in the ground next to the hand-size seedling with the date and name. The history of the centre is a living chronicle that you can browse beneath the shade of the neem trees.

It all began in 1994 with 45 farmers. Meanwhile, bioRe® Tanzania cooperates with 2,054 registered farmers. However, unlike in India there are no individual contracts but a kind of family contract. The land areas in Tanzania – in comparison with India – are much vaster. Each farmer now has between two and three hectares that are cultivated with the help of the wide-ranging family. This is not without risks. "If only one of them doesn't work properly, we no longer have any organic cotton," emphasizes Patrick Hohmann.

Currently, Tanzania is Remei AG's most important growing area. Due to the GMO problems the bulk of the Indian harvest had to be sold off in the conventional market as loss-minimizing trade. Therefore, Remei AG mainly relies on the Tanzanian cotton. About 70 % of the organic cotton comes from the 26 villages in the Meatu District. Genetically modified cotton is not approved in Tanzania and it looks as though it will stay this way. That makes organic farming much simpler. Besides, Tanzania's climate is much more homogeneous than India. While there are dozens of cotton varieties to choose from in India, the Tanzanian state only approves a single variety: UKM08. The code refers to Tanzania's Ukiriguru Agricultural Research Institute, which bred the particularly high-yielding variety, and the year that the seed was released.

What is more, bioRe® Tanzania is fortunate to have a ginning mill on site. Here, the seeds, whose tiny fine hairs cling onto the fibres in the ripened cotton bolls, are separated in ginning machines straight after the harvest. Cotton is an agricultural product and is primarily cultivated in the world's economically underdeveloped regions. This makes it challenging to add value on site. For example, if there is a power outage the cotton must be transported for ginning to other regions that are further away. However, in Tanzania's Meatu District Nassor

Ali Farai has succeeded in running a ginnery right in the heart of the growing area. The ginning mill has also been expanded thanks to the reliable cotton orders from bioRe®. Farai creates jobs and prospects because running the ginning mill requires specialist employees and administrative staff. The local ginnery is also an excellent employer because the company aims to comply with the SA8000 international standard. This is based on the conventions of the International Labour Organization (ILO) and the United Nations (UN). Its objective is to improve workers' conditions, among other things, by ruling out child labour, by allowing trade unions, by banning forced or compulsory labour, by protecting health and safety at work and many other aspects. Despite the guaranteed order status, the business is fraught with major challenges for Farai, a businessman with Ottoman ancestry. There are repeated power failures in the region, which makes it incredibly difficult to deliver the orders quickly and punctually.

Growing organic cotton also presents problems in Tanzania. Climate change and the associated unpredictability of the weather or longer periods of drought are an ongoing challenge. This is where the work of the bioRe® Foundation comes in, by building wells and 'harvesting water'. The bioRe® Foundation has invested in vast concrete water tanks which are linked with the roof ducts of adjacent buildings. The water torrents during the rainy season can then be captured. A single tank can supply up to 300 people with clean drinking water for ten to eleven months. 'Water harvests' are more sensible than wells with pump levers because they do not affect the groundwater. Oddly, however, it is more difficult for the foundation to find sponsors for the water tanks than for the wells, although 'water harvests' are much more productive and ecologically sustainable. Obviously, the image of a woman at the well is more emotive than the relative ease of capturing water as it falls from the sky.

The foundation is also proactive in training the farmers about erosion control. The more arid the soil, the easier it is for the wind to blow away the fertile soil layer. Natural hedging made from branches and scrub not only acts as windbreaks, but also offers refuge for birds and insects and encourages biodiversity. Since 2017 trials have been ongoing with hand machines to help with the sowing. The machines do not plough up the soil but merely open a small channel, just as much as is required to plant the seeds in the soil. The results are promising. It started out with three machines and meanwhile 50 of these devices are in use. It is also worthwhile mentioning the brand-new stoves which help ensure that bioRe® cotton is CO_2 neutral. These stoves make life much easier for the women because they use far less firewood. Looking for firewood is a woman's job and it normally takes up a lot of time. This time can be put to better use for activities that increase the family income. Of course, consuming less firewood also means that more trees escape deforestation in the vicinity of the farmhouses, in turn, helping to maintain the groundwater level.

Every time that Patrick Hohmann visits Tanzania he travels from one farm to another to talk to the farmers and ask them about their experiences. Under the shade of a tree, plastic chairs are set out for him and other guests, for the overseas visitors and members of the bioRe® team. Hohmann shakes hands with his hosts. He also shows more deference by gripping the farmers' forearm – this is a usual sign of respect in almost all African countries. Then he takes a seat and falls silent. He lets the time pass, as though he must first take in the surrounding countryside, before the conversation can begin. Nothing happens. Everyone glances around a little. Ah, a new house was built. How are the stoves working? How is the cotton seed doing that was issued by the government? What are the prospects for the harvest, and the pests? What is the news in the family? There is some chatter and then another long and friendly silence.

You sense that Patrick Hohmann feels at home, that he understands the people here as they understand him.

Damian Jilangi, who has participated in the project since 1994, is pleased with the harvest. He could buy himself a motorbike, which offers him an invaluable service in this sparsely populated area, because it is easier for him to access his fields on the bike. And he can visit his relatives whenever he wants. He and his wife have eight children; three of whom are already married. One son studied at university and now works as a teacher. One daughter is studying at police college, while another daughter attends the secondary school. Two sons have become farmers like their father. The family wears their best clothes and enjoys reporting about their work for organic cotton over the past year: the sowing season lasts from November to early February, and then there is the short rainy season. The main rainy season lasts from March to mid-May. In May/June, it is now harvest time; the cotton is tied into bed sheets and loaded onto the ox carts for transport to the collection centres in the villages. In front of the bioRe® storehouses the quality is checked; the volume is weighed and the cotton is transferred to sacks. In the tiny office next door, finally after having signed a receipt the farmers receive cash wages for their hard work.

"How is it going with the new hand machine for sowing?" Hohmann is curious to know. The Tanzanian farmers recently started to sow in rows and not simply out of their hands. This increases the yield and makes the harvest easier. The Tanzanian agronomist Marco Paul is on hand to interpret. The local language is Swahili; Hohmann greets the farmers in their native language, but he relies on his team for a more serious conversation. "Good," replies Paul. "Jilangi needed much less seed than last year, but the machine is heavy and not so easy to manoeuvre." Hohmann nods thoughtfully. "So, it's too heavy," he says. "Tell him that we'll check if something can be done about that."

In the 1990s when Patrick Hohmann started out with organic cotton in Tanzania, one day he was out in the middle of a cotton field when he had a flash of inspiration. He imagined a number sequence: '100/2/10'. This came to mind almost from nowhere and with no other explanation than ten years from now because of organic cotton Hohmann would succeed in doubling the income of a hundred-thousand farmers. "In India, I didn't achieve this," he says. "But I did succeed in Tanzania." In India, the GMO problems slowed down progress.

People approach Hohmann wherever he goes in the growing area in Meatu and ask him for interest-free loans. Tanzanians are pro-active and always have more business ideas. For example, a cooperative received an interest-free loan from the bioRe® Foundation to set up and run an oil mill. As mentioned, sunflowers grow in every cotton field. One day, the farmers had the idea of earning additional income by processing the sunflower seeds into cooking oil. The remainder of the pressed kernels make tasty and nutritious cattle feed that can also be sold. Hohmann comments admiringly, "With the exception of USD 250, the cooperative has repaid the loan in full."

Next to the oil mill is a wooden fence, which is surrounded by benches and shaded by a blue plastic tarpaulin. Behind the fence a woman cooks chicken and maize in two pots. This is a small restaurant for customers who visit the oil mill and for the farmers who deliver the cotton nearby. The restaurateur is successful. The benches are well occupied. She asks Hohmann whether the foundation could not award her a loan. She would love to have a permanent roof canopy that withstands the wind. Hohmann observes her restaurant and walks around the fence. "Did you build the fence yourself?" "Yes," the woman replies, she built it all by herself, without any help from the men. Hohmann hesitates. He seems to deliberate whether this would be assistance for a private individual, or whether the restaurant makes a contribution for the good of the village community. The foundation provides no funding for private individuals. Hohmann neither says yes nor no. It is not his responsibility to make a decision about loans. These are awarded by the Tanzanian bioRe® Foundation. Hohmann smiles and remains cautious. Once he commented, "I always maintain my distance, from royalty the same as from farmers." He then mentions the bioRe® co-worker Justina Samson and everyone knows her in this area anyway. "You can contact Justina," says Hohmann to the chef. "She will help you to write an application."

Remei AG, the bioRe® Foundation and bioRe® Labels

Why are things so complicated?

It is difficult for outsiders to find their bearings in Patrick Hohmann's business universe. It is not easy to appreciate the synergy between Remei AG and the bioRe® Foundation which at first seems complicated. However, it is worth reconsidering the cooperation between the limited company and the foundation precisely because it highlights an alternative way of production that is based on shared initiative rather than on competition.

Reticent and uncomprehending banks

Remei AG is a classic profit-oriented trading and textile company. Remei's executive board decided in 2004 that its future offer for retail customers should be exclusively organic cotton and finished organic cotton textiles. Patrick Hohmann followed his inner conviction. "You cannot do organic by halves," explains Hohmann, who found it more and more difficult to deal with organic cotton alongside conventionally produced cotton that is treated with pesticides and genetically modified. This corporate decision meant volunteering to halve company turnover, because the demand for organic cotton was not high enough to compensate for the loss of revenue from the traditionally produced cotton. The decision underlines that profit may be important for Hohmann, yet profit maximization is not his top priority. He has a critical attitude towards the accumulation of money. Entrepreneurial profit is only reasonable for him, if it serves the purpose of assuring continuity. Financial objectives are not Patrick Hohmann's paramount concern, but rather the opportunity to provide a humane livelihood for farmers in Tanzania and India, for the workers in supplier firms as well as to create scope for development. In practice, Remei AG is satisfied with annual profits of 2 to 3%. This is particularly modest, and it occasionally causes problems with the banks that authorize loans only if the rate of return on equity is at least 12%. In fact, this is counterproductive, since bank loans should stimulate and support the economy. Instead, they reward profit-maximizing behaviour. "I have to exploit the farmers, so that I can obtain a loan," is Patrick Hohmann's laconic summary. His conclusion is "a bank cannot give you a loan, if you need one." That was the case in 2018 when Remei AG faced a liquidity shortfall. There was a genuinely positive reason for this. The organic farmers in Tanzania had produced a bumper harvest and suddenly six-digit premiums were due for payment – a much higher sum than the previous year. Premiums are paid in cash to the farmers after their cotton delivery to the collection centres. However, Remei AG can only recoup the money once the ginned raw cotton is sold, that is, several months after the premiums have been paid out.

The bank refused a bridging loan simply because it failed to understand Patrick Hohmann's business model. Why should a company voluntarily forego profit to channel it to the weaker business partners? This makes no sense at all to the bank. Yet, this is precisely what Remei AG does: the company in Rotkreuz diverts 20 % of its annual profit to the bioRe® Foundation. Generally, this involves six-figure contributions every year. In turn, the foundation invests the money in the Indian and Tanzanian growing areas and funds projects that promote organic farming, as well as organizing infrastructure schemes in the fields of education, nutrition, health and agriculture.

Clothes with a feel good factor

Remei AG is not the only source of the foundation's financial resources. The aim is for the company's purchasers, i.e. the customers that buy the organic cotton and organic textiles to make a contribution and accept co-responsibility for the trading model of collaborative partnership. The retailer Coop is a crucial investor and the ideal patron of projects set up by the bioRe® Foundation. "I must persuade my purchasers not to worry too much about one-sided monetary payment, so they sell a garment not merely comprising price, but clothing that is all about human warmth and well-being," explains Patrick Hohmann, who sets great store by integrating the human factor into the production cycle. "My intention is not to produce garments for myself. I don't want to produce clothing for the customers. I want to produce clothes that epitomize the interaction between the farmers and the customers." Hohman gives a shrewd laugh, "I think I am getting there."

This observation sheds light on an obvious, though amazing fact: the farmers and consumers have never met one another. Usually, the farmers have never handled a T-shirt which was created from their cotton. In any case, they could not afford the product of their labour. To celebrate 25 years of cooperation with the Indian farmers, in November 2018 the Indian bioRe® Foundation held a small award ceremony under the village trees in Ajandi, Madhya Pradesh. As the farmers were presented with a special T-shirt made from their Namaskaar cotton, their deep emotion was tangible. As consumers, on the other hand, we are only aware of a small part of what goes into producing beautiful fabrics. Basically, we prefer to block out the unpleasant reality that the processes of making our clothing are tremendously complicated and massively underpaid. As soon as you begin to think about this, you only have two options: either to embrace fair trade and sustainable textiles or to endure sleepless nights.

The bioRe® sustainability labels

The bioRe® Foundation, established in 1997, performs another important role: it presides over the award of the sustainability labels known as bioRe® Sustainable Cotton and bioRe® Sustainable Textiles. Fashion brands rely on these to demonstrate a high standard of sustainable textiles to their customers. The foundation is independent. This gives an assurance that no compromises are made on the ambitious ethical and ecological goals, for example, if Remei AG were to plan to relax the trading standards to do more lucrative business. The separate decision-making powers make it feasible to safeguard against such temptations.

Another innovation of this kind was introduced in 2004. This was the year when bioRe® India Ltd., bioRe® Tanzania Ltd. and both their associated foundations officially belonged to the farmers. In other words, more responsibility was delegated to the local qualified experts. The members of the foundation boards in India and Tanzania are represented by Indian or Tanzanian specialists who have the autonomy to decide which projects are reasonable in light of the foundations' objectives. This creates a level playing field for the partnership. The bioRe® Foundation approves the funds, as long as they are in accordance with its mission.

Patrick Hohmann is keen for the structure of the organizations he has set up to be based on sustainability. Given that the bioRe® companies are not classic subsidiaries of Remei AG, they have more autonomy and independence. Even in the event of Remei AG's bankruptcy, they would retain full legal trading rights. If it seems reasonable for bioRe® India Ltd. and bioRe®

Tanzania Ltd., they can trade independently of Remei AG. Naturally, this is always with the caveat that the business activities should coincide with the foundation's objectives. For example, bioRe® India Ltd. launched a scheme to sell organic vegetables. Planting the organic cotton in crop rotation means that organic vegetables are also produced. The farmers so far sold their vegetables at the local markets, yet they had no opportunity to gain the added value of organic certification. In Madhya Pradesh, people earn so little that almost no one could pay extra for organic vegetables. However, a wealthy middle class lives in India's big cities and they are easily prepared to pay double the price. Many in the middle and upper classes studied in the US or England where they became familiar with organic products. Besides, the problem of pesticides is certainly a subject of public debate. This encourages a market for Indian organic vegetables and bioRe® India Ltd. has the freedom to supply this market. Although Patrick Hohmann and his team had to cope with countless setbacks in India, it has still been possible to launch successful projects that generate added value for the participating farmers.

P. 119, top | **The handloom project Aavran Handlooms on site at bioRe® India Ltd. provides women with a supplementary income. The independent company produces traditional, handwoven scarves and table linen. Hand weaver, Kiran Bhalse, is seen in the photo**

P. 119, bottom | **The bioRe® Foundation funds biogas plants that use the cow dung from the farms as raw material. The biogas is utilized for cooking. This avoids the time-consuming search for firewood and heating. The women have more time for themselves, their children and for money-making activities. Here, Kanti Yadav cooks for her family.**

Top | **Patrick Hohmann at one of the "Open House Days" in India. Overseas visitors get a warm welcome at the bioRe® projects. Conversely, Tanzanian and Indian project participants have the opportunity to travel to Europe to find out about the destination for the organic cotton.**

Top right | **The "animation schools" were set up because the state schools are inaccessible for the children in the growing area.**

Bottom right | **Meanwhile, 1,200 children attend the bioRe® schools in Madhya Pradesh. The schools are open to all children, not only the farmers' children. In November 2018 the first youngsters received their graduation diplomas, a sensation in an area where education is notoriously underdeveloped.**

bioRe

Bottom | **The girls and women collect water for the large families. Sometimes, there is a spare a hand cart, but they often carry home the full bucket on their heads. To shorten the trips, the bioRe® Foundation is building wells and large water tanks, where rainwater is captured and can be stored for up to nine months.**

Top right | **The bioRe® Training Centre in the Nimar Valley in Kasrawad. The farmers, increasingly women farmers, attend training courses here about organic farming.**

Bottom right | **A specially equipped bioRe® medical bus supplies patients in remote areas with high-quality medical care like e.g. ultrasound, blood tests, X-ray etc. In the photo, Jyoti Karma, (Pathology Technician).**

EMERGENCY EXIT

Transparency and re-traceability from the finished garment to the farmer

---

"We don't exclusively rely on the certificates."

On the face of it, it hardly sounds so adventurous to aspire to hang in the wardrobe a piece of sustainable fashion that pays a fair wage to all producers. It is a simple ambition but living up to it is complex. Moreover, it goes hand in hand with the absurdities of an uncontrolled industry. Cotton is too cheap for one thing. Many countries, especially the USA and European states, subsidize cotton growing and therefore cause artificially cheapened surplus capacities. The revenue from cotton no longer covers the growing costs. Subsidies introduce a market distortion, so the cotton price is not a true reflection of the effort invested in growing the white raw material. Patrick Hohmann already noticed a lack of true-cost pricing in the early 1990s when the cotton price was still about USD 1 per kilogram. In the meantime, there is even greater disparity between the effort and the rewards due to the continually falling cotton price whose current value is USD 0.72 per kilogram for conventional cotton.

Sustainable textiles have to hold their own in this situation. Basically, it is a contest between slow fashion and fast fashion because the continual downward pricing pressure inspires short-lived trends. Fashion is cheap. The consumers buy clothes more often than they need to. Marie Kondo, the renowned Japanese tidying expert, clearly shows on Netflix how consumers compulsively fill their wardrobes. This seems to have little to do with the pleasure derived from buying a beautiful garment. Setting an alternative fashion trend is not easy for a company. Remei already has the challenge of managing the volume of cotton that is grown. Markus Kunz, who is in charge of Remei's supply management and controlling system, explains: "It takes three years for conventional farmers to convert to organic crops. Therefore, we have to predict market trends for at least three years and to estimate how many farmers can contract to supply the bioRe® companies. Since we give the farmers a purchase guarantee and pay a premium of 15% on top of the market price for the organic cotton, we cannot afford to produce surplus capacities. We can only fund the purchase guarantee and premium by selling finished products. Of course, to be on the safe side we always grow slightly more cotton than we need just to ensure that we maintain delivery capacity." Remei's annual harvest is about 2000 tonnes of ginned organic cotton, and almost 1,000 tonnes are earmarked for their own value-added chain. About 500 tonnes can be sold externally as organic cotton. And because the demand for organic cotton is not so high, a further 500 tonnes are supplied to the conventional market. The sale of these 500 tonnes is a purely loss-minimizing transaction. On this basis, the additional work for the sustainable cultivation cannot be compensated for by earning more revenue: the high-quality organic cotton is sold at the price of conventional cotton.

"When I retired from Coop," says Jürg Peritz, "I had the first chance to review Remei AG's accounts. Financing and planning processes are among Patrick Hohmann's strengths as a businessman. I am incredibly impressed by the professional way that this is done at Remei." In practice, Remei AG has put in place a controlling system with the guarantee of meeting the sustainability targets across all production processes. This is a considerable achievement because Remei works with about

35 suppliers from all over the world, i.e. ginning factories and spinning mills in India and Tanzania as well as companies in India, Tanzania and Lithuania, which produce cotton cloths from the yarn, as well as dyeing, accessorizing, printing, tailoring and finishing.

The raw material and the semi-finished products are transported on long journeys across several continents. It is always important to monitor the smooth flow of the merchandise and to check that the delivered products have been genuinely processed. Is the organic cotton at a factory clearly marked as organic material? Is the product stored in different warehouses and correctly separated from the conventional cotton? If melange yarn is spun from white and grey cotton-fibre flocks, does this genuinely contain the black fibre as specified in Remei's chemical formulas? These sorts of questions must be answered. Remei has therefore developed a re-traceability system, whereby every batch and every work phase has an ID number. Remei's partners are fully compliant with this system. "Re-traceability ensures that you can always tell the truth. Only those who promise transparency can also guarantee authenticity," according to Patrick Hohmann. "Of course, it's still possible that mishaps occur, which is exactly why we carry out the checks." The consumers also have the chance to verify the retraceability because every garment with Remei's bioRe® Sustainable Textiles label has a barcode to confirm the supply chain. What about the risk of disclosing confidential commercial information? After all, the industry usually keeps supplier addresses as a jealously guarded secret. Markus Kunz, who is a qualified atmospheric physicist and environmental scientist, says no. "Actually, we would like others to copy us," he explains with a smile.

Remei sets itself high and holistic standards that go beyond the usual industry norms such as the Global Organic Textile Standard (GOTS), the best-known standard for sustainably produced textiles. GOTS mainly focuses on the use of certified organic cotton and its ecological processing. Its rationale is the use of officially recognized certification records. However, it provides no information about the prior phase, i.e. organic cotton cultivation and especially the conditions for organic cotton farmers. Yet, this is precisely Patrick Hohmann's vital interest. His life's work is devoted to improving the situation for farmers, since he is convinced that only sustainable agriculture, whose achievements are valued and correspondingly rewarded, will promote social well-being. We previously mentioned that Remei upholds the following values: organic cotton, fair trade, ecological and skin-friendly, CO_2 neutral and re-traceability back to the growers. As no existing model standardized these values for all phases from cultivation to the finished garment, bioRe® Sustainable Textiles was launched and defined as an independent standard. This innovation is unprecedented.

There are several recognized standards that apply prior to and for the stage of ginned cotton. Therefore, the bioRe® Foundation has appointed Flocert – a subsidiary company of Fair Trade International – to audit its bioRe® Sustainable Cotton label. Nonetheless, it is down to Remei to vouch for the other production stages. The industry approach is to address such complicated challenges by obtaining certificates to assure the quality of every element of the production phase. Remei on the other hand follows its own principles and observes its standards of ecological production, social well-being and transparency for its entire supply chain from the cotton fibre to the finished textile.

bioRe® Sustainable Textiles is justifiably acknowledged as the highest international standard for organic cotton textiles. Remei notably encourages its partners to comply with the

SA8000 norm that endorses the conventions of the International Labour Organization (ILO) and the United Nations. However, the SA8000 norms not only address working conditions, minimum wages and safety at work. They also integrate social values into the management process. "Our partners had a positive experience with this," says Markus Kunz. "I recently spoke to an Indian partner who is SA8000-certified. He told me that many of the ideas about safety at work or productivity come from the workers themselves. And as a business manager, it is often easier for him to communicate by liaising with the workers' representatives." Marion Röttges, co-managing director of Remei, confirms the benefits of SA8000: "It is a completely different attitude whether the impetus for progress comes proactively from management, or whether an inspector turns up who just gets a snapshot of things. SA8000 puts the onus on companies to define a policy, to analyze their objectives and outcomes and to keep records about the progress. We base our work with our production partners on this kind of continual development."

Remei also treats sustainability as a dynamic process. The company constantly strives to improve its own standards. "We aim to give the auditors the opportunity to suggest improvements," explains Markus Kunz. To begin with, such ecological aspects were tackled as child labour, then 'detox' in dyeing and the closed water circulation system. Finally, CO_2 neutrality was addressed. The company's carbon footprint is now neutral. This is quite an achievement in the transport-intensive textile industry. Carbon offsetting proved possible due to almost 3,000 biogas plants at Indian farms. They use cow manure to generate fuel for stoves which offset about 7,000 tonnes of CO_2. At this point, things come full circle again between the finished textile product and the farmer at the start of the production process. Markus Kunz currently concentrates on human rights aspects and the potential for a common standard across the entire textile chain. Occasionally, this creates some headaches because there are already different calculation methods for the farmers' subsistence income and wages for textile workers. Furthermore, Remei has an ambitious plan to pay the sewers a subsistence wage. The company also hopes that this will apply for all other professional groups within the manufacturing process. However, this goes beyond the usual remit. Markus Kunz has already formulated a policy to ensure that the five principles that Remei stands for are verifiable on an ongoing basis. He is confident that at the latest by the end of 2020 the company will have achieved a standard for its bioRe® Sustainable Textiles label that is audited by an independent third party. "We know that we have a good label and that people trust us; but we need an agency to award us the certification." Remei would then be the first and only company worldwide whose entire textile chain is recognized as sustainable and fair.

Although the company goes to great lengths to comply with high standards and to gain assurances for these, Patrick Hohmann is convinced that self-responsibility is ultimately what matters the most. "We see the certifications as a means to help us meet our obligations. That sets us apart from other suppliers who treat everything as trouble-free, as long as the papers are in order. However, we don't exclusively rely on the certificates. As soon as we have the slightest inkling that something is not right with our cotton, we look into the matter." This is also necessary because the integrity of the certifications fluctuates from one country to another. Remei sends assessors from Switzerland to the production areas whenever it can. However, not all countries authorize this. For example, in India the government requires local inspectors to carry out certification checks. “We take our standards very seriously,” explains Markus Kunz regarding the certifications. However, he also mentions a key aspect on all levels at Remei. “The best situation is to be personally present on site as often as possible, to cultivate relationships with the people in the production factories and to talk to each other to clarify where there is potential to improve something.”

Letting Go of a Life's Work

"There are always individuals who are willing to take over the reins."

Patrick Hohmann is now aged 68 and he has a rich store of experience. He has clearly left his mark on the company that he established as well as the foundation that evolved from his business. Having progressed from a yarn and cotton dealer to a producer of organic cotton, he finally identified the spinning mills that could make yarn from this organic cotton that he sold. He was lucky to find reliable partners in Jürg Peritz and Coop and he gradually transformed the entire production process so that sustainability lies at the heart of everything from the designs to the dyeing process, printing, cutting, tailoring, accessorizing with buttons and zips, packaging and supply. Remei nowadays sees itself as a holistic provider of solutions for sustainable textiles production. The bioRe® Foundation assures unrivalled ecological and social standards thanks to its quality labels. It is also instrumental in promoting the well-being of the farmers, their families, the village community and nature conservation. "Fair trade means that another person earns enough beyond life's necessities so that he has space to develop." That is Patrick Hohmann's definition. Ever the pragmatist, he cleverly adds, "Fairness also means that everyone is a bit happy and unhappy at the same time." While Patrick Hohmann may be a successful businessman who has established an alternative business model to counteract the Goliath of an overbearing industry, he certainly never promised anyone a rose garden.

The challenging plan for a successor

Of course, the question is how the future is mapped out for a company that is dependent on the charisma of its founder's personality. How will things work out at Remei and the bioRe® Foundation when one day Patrick Hohmann completely steps back? What will it be like? "Different," comments Hohmann laconically. "Individuality cannot be replicated like a production series, but there are always individuals who are willing to take over the reins."

Patrick Hohmann was not always such an optimist. In 2009 he suffered multiple organ failure after he contracted sepsis. After three weeks in a coma and six weeks in the general ward fighting for his life, he realized that he urgently needed to make arrangements for his successor. Hohmann's eldest son, Patrick Hohmann Jr, was already keen to take over early on. "Surely, any father would be delighted for his son to take an interest in the business that he has built up?" comments Elisabeth Hohmann on this subject. Patrick Hohmann Jr is a qualified business manager who had a successful career as marketing director for a technology company where he was in charge of some important projects. He was already a member of the board of directors at Remei AG as well.

Patrick Hohmann Jr had recently accomplished a major project, yet without informing his father he resigned from his job at the technology firm. His dream was to set up his own company specializing in the production of luxury watches using space rocket debris. Hohmann Jr, who is an adventurer like his father, travelled for weeks through the Kazakh steppe to purchase debris from Russian Soyuz rockets. He survived endless vodka orgies; he was suspected of being a Western spy and encountered shady businessmen. In the end, he succeeded in buying parts of Soviet and Russian rockets and transporting them back to Switzerland. The watch brand was launched when Patrick Hohmann Sr summoned his wife and four children to a meeting with the solicitor to mutually agree the company's future. Patrick Hohmann Sr now commissioned an assessment. "What happened was bound to happen. My father gave me an ultimatum," Patrick Hohmann Jr writes in his autobiographical novel "Werenbach's Watch". "Either to be his successor, or Werenbach. I wasn't prepared for this."[5] When his son suggested to Patrick Hohmann that he would carry on marketing his space watch as a hobby alongside his work as Remei CEO, his father decided on a different solution. "I noticed that he was passionate about the watch and that he should really do that." This was a painful moment for both men. The young entrepreneur missed the opportunities that he had prepared for thanks to his training and the course of his career. His father was worn down by the guilt of not having appointed his son as the company's new chief executive, the position that he always had in mind for him. An external successor was brought on board for the role in 2015. He seemed to take the company forward at first, but then the culture of dialogue was jeopardized at the head office and with the project teams in India and Tanzania. This culture was a crucial part of Remei's success. The company encountered a difficult phase.

Simon Hohmann

Two chief executives have been co-managing the company since April 2018. Simon Hohmann, Patrick Hohmann's secondeldest son, was appointed together with Marion Röttges, who has worked for Remei since 2004. Simon Hohmann, born in 1977, had always kept out of the discussions about the company succession. His career began with a commercial traineeship in the semiconductor industry. When he joined Remei back in 2003 he had previously worked in the export department of a medical technology company. At Remei, he began in the garments division and completed continuing education with the Swiss diploma in business management. "I wasn't so interested in whether a T-shirt has this blue or a slightly different colour, and whether the blue now contains more or less yellow. I couldn't get very enthusiastic about textile design at the outset," admits Simon Hohmann. In fact, he had intended to leave his father's company again, when his father reminded him that there would soon be a vacancy as the new manager of the yarn department. Maybe that was something to interest him? "Ernst Ehrismann was the manager of yarn trading. He was a very good person; I enjoyed working with him," recalls Simon Hohmann. He took over when Ehrismann retired, but he always declined when his father and brother mentioned running the company. "My father was unlucky that the one son in the business wasn't interested in taking over. Perhaps, it would have been a lot easier if back in 2003 I had already said: I'll do it." In 2013 Simon Hohmann left the company to start a job as sales manager for a manufacturer of technical sealing components. He also studied for an MBA from the Lucerne University of Applied Sciences and Arts. With the benefit of an outside perspective, he began to appreciate what actually defined Remei's culture. "When I was twenty years old, I couldn't relate either to organic or fair trade cotton. Now, I'm forty and I am interested in it. Who knows? Maybe when I'm sixty, I'll also take an interest in anthroposophy," says Simon Hohmann.

Simon Hohmann is currently the product manager for cotton and yarn. His specialist interests are business management, financial calculation and pricing. He appreciates that Remei also entertains ideas that are not about economic efficiency and profit. He has great respect for the social side of his new position as co-managing director. "The areas where one-plus-one do not necessarily make two are the organic projects, fair trade and the social aspects. These issues are often involved in a conflict of objectives which influences our day-to-day business. If you make an error in this system and focus on the wrong objective, this has an enormous impact. Ultimately, thousands of people depend on us. I wouldn't have wanted to become the boss on my own. Then, the idea came up for a co-chief executive solution together with Marion, which is a very good solution for me."

Marion Röttges

Marion Röttges, who qualified as a textile engineer at the University of Applied Sciences in Kaiserslautern (not in Reutlingen), is co-chief executive at Remei. She is in charge of the apparel and communication division. She is also clear about the immense complexity of the business model. "I cannot imagine one person single-handedly managing everything. The way that things usually work in the conventional textile trade is that a designer has an idea and places it with an agent. This idea then goes into production, regardless of the location, with the cheapest subcontractor. At Remei, we purchase the cotton with incredibly versatile uses for a specific range of textiles, though not for other types. We work in the sector of middle-staple cotton, i.e. the fibres have a staple length of between 22 and 29 millimetres, which can be used for most textiles. We would need very fine cotton textiles for long-staple cotton. During product development we already factor in the suitability of our cotton fibres for our customers' end products. From start to finish, you assume full responsibility. This is what makes everything so complex."

Marion Röttges knows what she is talking about. She worked for several years as a quality manager for a large, international retail group with headquarters in Zug. Three flight tickets were on her desk on Mondays and week in, week out she flew around the world to visit the production sites. She went to dyeing plants, finishing factories and tanneries. Marion Röttges saw first-hand the conditions in which people did their work here. She also witnessed the ecological collateral damage that was created due to the one-sided focus on price. The fashion industry directly or indirectly employs one in six people around the world. This sector causes the most environmental pollution after the oil industry. 80 billion items of clothing are produced every year; this is 400% per cent more than 20 years ago. If you bear in mind that in the 1960s people still mainly wore clothes that were produced in their local neighbourhood, you get an idea of the scale of the ecological and social costs.[6]

In 2003 Marion Röttges became pregnant. Her employer's procurement division relocated from Zug to Hong Kong. It was clear that she no longer wanted to work in the conventional textile industry. "I always wondered why you specialize in procurement for a company that produces things in a way that you would never like to work yourself. I wouldn't want to stand in a tannery in bare feet. I wouldn't like to work in a textile printing plant without protective clothing or to sandblast jeans. However, I was working in a system where that is exactly what you expected of people. The buyers rarely concentrated on the details of reasonable production because their day-to-day reality was that today they were buying clothes, tomorrow shoes and kitchen utensils the next day."

The strongest incentive for unfair trade under the capitalist model, in addition to pricing pressure, is the conventional division of work into many different processes that no one can completely oversee. The breakdown of jobs into micro-tasks leads to the focus on the task at hand, so depersonalizing the work processes. How can I be responsible for the larger scale, if my job is just to sew on trouser buttons? Why should it be urgent for me to work as part of a team to stop the destructive side of an industry, if my daily focus is a small, specialized task? Machiavelli's motto was "divide and conquer". The capitalist approach relies not merely on this principle in dealing with people, but also in breaking down the work processes to destroy the sense of responsibility.

Clarifying and untangling responsibilities

Marion Röttges made a phone call to Patrick Hohmann when she heard about him. In his characteristic way, he also recruited her. He set a new precedent in his company by creating a brand-new position for Marion Röttges: she started work as a quality manager at Remei a few months after giving birth to her first child. Hohmann already hinted during their initial conversations that he regarded her as an eligible candidate for his successor. However, Röttges could not envisage this, especially not in Switzerland where child care is a challenge for every family. Nevertheless, she was willing to take on responsibility. She helped to get a clear picture of the accountabilities and overall to make the company less dependent solely on Patrick Hohmann. This also meant untangling the association of Remei and the bioRe® Foundation, whose operational business is meanwhile overseen by its managing director Christa Suter.

A new era can begin

Both Simon Hohmann and Marion Röttges are optimistic about the future. Although less organic cotton is grown today than a few years ago, they agree that this presents no risk for their business model. "The wheat is just separating from the chaff," comments Simon Hohmann on current market developments. "The surviving companies will be the ones to take things seriously and produce organic cotton on principle. The broad masses, which produce fake organic cotton, will drop out because the topic is too hot for retail businesses. They don't want to risk damage to their reputation with merchandise that is not impeccable." The major fashion brands, which are high street names in every city centre, temporarily used high-profile advertising campaigns for their 'organic cotton' collections. However, in the meantime, the message has been heavily scaled back, although few details were released by the respective companies. However, trade experts believe that the organic cotton from mass market brands proved to be GMO-contaminated, so the major players became extremely cautious.

Marion Röttges, like Simon Hohmann, is convinced that a growing potential group of consumers is interested in sustainable textiles. Yet, she recognizes too that it will not be straightforward to find decision-makers and attract brands for the bioRe® quality seal of sustainability over the longer term. "We're in a market where the general idea is that 'organic cotton' is easy. The trade fairs that we attend are booming. Sustainable fashion is on trend. The pretence is that there are simple solutions. You already wonder sometimes why we find things so difficult when everybody else seems to find it so easy." Röttges sees the biggest challenge due to immense trading changes as people switch to online shopping, and she believes that Remei has to chaperone its customers throughout this process. In this case, communicating the bioRe® sustainability credentials could become problematic because this relies on constant fact-sharing. However, this is part of the social media context and its perpetual tendency to reduce people's attention span as well as the diminished role of vertical knowledge. Nevertheless, Marion Röttges has no doubt about one thing, “The heyday of carefree global textile acquisition is over. We will find people who are keen to source what we do. They will appreciate us.”

“THE LIVING HEDGE” OF MEINRAD INGLIN

Patrick Hohmann on His Favourite Short Story ("The Living Hedge")

A book that you often bring up in conversation and frequently quote is the short story entitled "The Living Hedge" ("Der Lebhag") by the Swiss writer Meinrad Inglin (1893–1971). How did you come across this book?

School didn't interest me at all. The only interesting thing about school was the break times. I wanted to finish the Matura school-leaving certificate with the least possible work. I knew that my German teacher was an expert on Meinrad Inglin. So, I thought it was a good idea to suggest something by Meinrad Inglin as a text for the Matura exam. I decided on the "Grand Hotel Excelsior" and I browsed a few of the short texts by Meinrad Inglin. I simply looked for the shortest story that I could find by Meinrad Inglin and that was "The Living Hedge". I instantly liked it, but at the time I didn't think any more about the story's content. It was not till later that I realized there is a connection between the text and my work. I have been re-reading "The Living Hedge" for decades, and my affinity with this story goes deeper and deeper. I discover something new every time I read it.

What intrigues you about this text?

"The Living Hedge": I think the title alone is sensational. When you destroy the environment, the social structure falls apart. Sustainable agriculture promotes social well-being. This short story describes it exactly. The hedge is destroyed, erosion affects the land and domestic bliss disappears. The children are no longer interested, the parents argue and grandfather becomes bad-tempered. The story shows how a tiny change can have profound effects.

Do you regard "The Living Hedge" as a metaphor for man's relationship with nature?

We need the relationship with nature as well as human relationships. In Switzerland, for example, there are farmers who have no relationship whatsoever to the soil, but they only keep farming because of the subsidies. The effect is that the social environment is also money-oriented. It is noticeable that the social context is still intact around organic farmers. Farming with bigger and bigger fields is not working. On the contrary, you need small organisms that can coexist. In Inglin's story, the living hedge is one of these small organisms. The hedge on its own ensures that the family has a good life together.

In Tanzania, there is no fence around the bioRe® Centre. Did you get this idea from "The Living Hedge"?

There is no point fencing in land. That only means that everyone else has to continue living in poverty. If you think about Europe, you draw this conclusion. We don't want others to have a share in our development. Quite the opposite, we make sure that they carry on being poor, so that we can stay rich. This is the wrong approach in my opinion. We definitely have to create spaces, so people all over the world can develop. Tariff agreements with minimum prices are not the right way. This only leads us to focus on money and justifies the desire to continue buying things at cheaper and cheaper prices.

You once mentioned the importance of the 'invisible forces': what exactly do you mean by this?

Take homeopathy, for example: you cannot prove why it works, but it does. Or the soil condition: we don't know 80% of the micro-organisms, but they are effective. When we examine the soil where genetically modified cotton is growing, we see big differences. We cannot measure them, but we observe the difference. Species diversity is vanishing more and more. If we want to live, then we have to give invisible forces a chance. "The living hedge" is another example of this kind of invisible force. Species diversity is alive!

"The Living Hedge" by Meinrad Inglin

On an exposed, mountain plain with sparsely growing trees the farmers had uprooted all the hedges with the exception of one, and they enclosed their fields and meadows with lifeless iron posts and wire fences. They claimed that these fences were more convenient and neater, that they took away no light from the soil and required no additional work. They seemed to be indifferent that the land now looked bleaker; they were concerned about the land's use, not its beauty, which was why they were farmers.

The last green hedge owed its survival to old Boniface who wanted to keep it, and he set to work with his hedge shears to prune back its prolific growth every year. His son, Blasius, who was known as Bläsi, would have replaced it long ago with a wire fence and he only reluctantly gave way to his obstinate father. The land plot was triangular. The western half was meadowland, while crops were grown in sections of the eastern half. The two-storey, brown wooden house, with adjoining stable and barn, stood between the two halves. The hedge on the north-facing, long side marked the boundary of the farmstead from the neighbour's meadow. This neighbour had also suggested a wire fence, but he had made do without it up till now because old Boniface saved him the work with the hedge shears.

The hedge was thick and flourishing with hawthorn, field maple, dogwood and other perennial shrubs; it was overgrown with bindweed and hops, flowers and animals thrived at its feet, a real living hedge. When the late-cut hay was gathered from the meadow and the harvest was brought in from the field, one sunny day in autumn old Boniface walked sedately along the hedgerow from early morning to late evening. He frugally smoked a pipe with a cover that hung down into his grey beard; his tanned bald head was shining, and his eyes glanced kind-heartedly over the undergrowth where he knew every single shrub. Thorn shoots, leafy twigs and tall branches tumbled over his powerful shears that he worked with calmly and uniformly. Birds often flew out of the thicket in front of him only to fly back in again a short way ahead, and he hummed reassuringly. A hare leapt out from under his feet and, laughing, he watched as he sped off with pricked-up ears and found his hiding place in the foliage. Sometimes, it seemed as if several hazel rods suddenly began to dance and move away from him. "Heavens above!" he cried aloud. "The hedge is jumping away from me!" He walked after the hazel branches and rattled the shears, until behind the hedge the giggling grew louder to a delighted scream and the children appeared.

The children, one boy and two girls, were allowed to play on the whole of the meadow after it had been mowed or grazed, yet they preferred to brush along the hedge, to hide in it and make discoveries or to loiter in its shade on hot summer days. The hedge was and continued to be their paradise, even when they went to school. Only here, and nowhere in their surroundings, did they find the first primroses, wood anemones and violets. The hawthorn came into flower a little later and it appeared in some places as though snowflakes had been deposited on the clipped green hedge. The hedge now began to burst into bud everywhere and grandfather Boniface showed the children the wonderful new shoots on the sturdy maple branches that he had trimmed back short and bare. He carefully guided them to a bird's nest that they should protect; they once showed him a nest, too, a round, firm nest made from green moss with a bolt-hole, the home of the wren. In May, grandfather collected the stems at the end of the thin coarse hops branches, which were already trailing precariously above the hedge, and he fried them with butter in a pan to make some tender vegetables. Blossoming among the thorns were privet, honeysuckle and woodbine, and in the summer at the hedge margins tall meadowsweet, columbine and other flowers came into bloom that were not found anywhere else on the meadow. The hedge was so high in August that a grown man could no longer peer above it; it gleamed in October with its variegated foliage beneath the deep blue sky, as though it had gathered upon it all the colours of autumn. There were still plenty of creatures, animals and plants, which found a last safe refuge here, although they remained hidden or unknown. Only old Boniface knew that they were there, and he rejoiced at the thought.

A cold, wet autumn arrived, and grandfather withdrew with a long illness. Bläsi and his neighbour neither had the time nor the desire to nurture the living hedge themselves, so they decided to uproot it instead. They set to work in the wintertime. They brandished a pick axe, cursed and laboured for days; the hedge with its thick roots was tough and caused them more trouble than had they taken turns to tend it for ten winters. The children looked on ruefully. "It's a real shame!" said the older girl, but her father replied that it was high time to pull out the abandoned undergrowth, weeds and bugs.

When grandfather finally recovered in the summertime and went outdoors with his stick, instead of his living hedge he only saw an iron fence. He said not a word. Rather, he stared for a long time as though he could not comprehend it and the joy of his cheerful old age was extinguished from his gaze. He had been the good spirit of the house, and now he grew sullen and frail. “The illness has taken it out of him,” said his family. They did not imagine that less than an illness can forever upset an old man who is accustomed to his lifelong habits.

It was the children who missed the living hedge the most. They no longer took pleasure in hurrying back from school because something was absent at home that had once enticed them. Whenever they played in their free time, they grew tired of the game sooner than before at the inexhaustible hedge. Grandfather could not show them things any longer; he found no real reason to spend time with them. Their yearning for the hedge was short-lived; they eventually even forgot about it in the healthy way that children do. But the forcible destruction of their paradise had also deprived them a little of their joy of life, a precious affinity that they lacked in the times ahead. They were no longer so cheerful as before, although they did not know it.

Myriads of birds had always lived in the hedge; tits, robins and wrens and occasionally a chiffchaff, a red-backed warbler. They fed on the insects and destroyed more of them than a farmer would ever suspect on his land and soil. The birds had now disappeared, and they no longer came back; they lived only in the woodlands and hedgerows where they found protection. The small bugs thrived even better from this point on; they are only visible to the human eye when they start to cause damage. The pests reared their brood that could overwinter on the tree without any danger. The potato crop was ravaged by a previously scarcely known and dangerous beetle. Leaf cockroaches, gnats, caterpillars and all kinds of larvae thrived unhindered. Bläsi was surprised the whole year long about one thing and another, about the torn flowers, branches stripped bare, gnawed potato plants and worm-eaten fruit. But that was only the beginning; the pests multiplied from year to year and the harvest deteriorated, while the frustration grew and grew.

Hedgehogs had lived in the hedge and they ate the grubs and insects on their night-time forays. The hedgehogs no longer had anywhere to hide, and they moved to a place where there were still hedges. A weasel family did the same, for at last they had been chased from their hiding holes beneath the hedge. These sleek and slender predators had killed off the field mice here year in, year out and pursued them relentlessly into their passageways. Now the mice rapidly multiplied and became a plague.

All of this was incomprehensible for Bläsi. He thought nothing more of it; he only did more or less what his neighbours had done too.

He was a harmless, good-natured man. Yet, he was almost always in a bad mood now and his family suffered because of it. However, the other farmers nearby had previously endured similar experiences, and they were not surprised that Bläsi also had his share of the general troubles.

Another dry, windy year followed with the direst consequences. The old people claimed that things had never looked so bad before in longer and windier dry seasons; living on the land was not a blessing any more. But now the open, sunny land was exploited down to the last few inches and there were neat wire fences. In the old days, the numerous hedges had blocked or weakened the desiccating wind, the warm soil humidity had been maintained and in the rainless weeks at least the nightly dew had humidified the soil. The wind presently swept over the land like it was a bare steppe and the sparse fruit trees no longer stopped it. The wind damaged the grass that failed to grow, being intolerant of windy conditions; it quickly dried out the dew and deprived the soil of the necessary warmth and moisture; it dusted away soil from the arid fields; it relentlessly puffed away the carbon dioxide from the base of the green planting cover that it absorbs to develop. It all came about in an extremely windy dry season, but it also happened in the dry summer weeks, albeit less noticeably, and the old, hallowed soil began to deteriorate.

One or the other scourge would have been tolerable. There would have been no reason to shout and search for the cause. However, it was unbearable to endure all these problems together. Bläsi thought that something was wrong. What other explanation could there be that from a certain year onwards the pests simultaneously ruined the flowers, leaves and fruits, that a plague of mice rummaged and gnawed everywhere and that growth was stunted on the fields and in the meadows!

You could see and more or less expect this kind of damage. However, another loss that afflicted Bläsi and his relatives was more difficult to detect and incalculable. It began with old Boniface's depression. Grandfather was also the good spirit of the house for a long while. It carried on with what seemed like the children's harmless disappointment, their quietly dwindling love of fun that they would have dearly needed later on. Then came Bläsi's rage against his misfortune, his perpetual bad mood, which also made his wife's life difficult. No one was content any longer in the house.

The other farmers had begun using machines and artificial fertilizers and spraying the insects with poison. Bläsi observed for a while, although in the end he found that it only cost money without helping a great deal. Besides, things had worked much better before without these artificial measures. He no longer thought it worthwhile to slave away and he started to neglect all kinds of things. "It's like everything is jinxed, nothing works!" he shouted. Because this was too much to bear, he started to drink cider and schnapps to forget about it.

His older daughter got married as soon as possible. His younger daughter hardly tolerated it much longer at home; she moved away and worked in a proper household where she liked it better. His son, whose apprenticeship was so harsh and who watched his father's bad example, lost all pleasure in farming. He disappeared one day. He wrote from somewhere else that he worked in a factory, so they might excuse him now; he had no need to toil to the bone, he had his free time here and earned a decent wage.

That was the day when Bläsi got drunk. When his wife scolded him, he became sorry for himself. He shouted that it was not his fault that everything had turned out wrongly. There was no blessing any longer and he didn't know why.

His wife was a steely, hard-working woman, yet she was no smarter than him. "We must pray for the blessing and go to church more often then," she responded. And she meant it. Bläsi raised no objection, because he was still a devout man despite everything.

Saying prayers and attending church helped both of them for a while to overcome their deepest dejection. However, the yields did not increase. When a man loses his appreciation for nature's wonder and beauty, so he acts less according to nature's divine wisdom than his own thoughts, thus despising or misusing the means that God puts in his hands, he will pray for help in all the churches of the world, but to no avail.

Bläsi carried on drinking and his wife often had to do all the work alone. When he came to the table one morning sober and in the foulest mood, she complained bitterly. He became coarse, and they began a loud argument. The woman did not bear it for long. She burst into tears; in despair, she turned to the old father, crying that things could truly not go on like this and that she didn't know what to do.

Grandfather Boniface, who was seated at the table, frail and trembling as he dipped his bread into the milky coffee, awoke from his apathy. He listened for a while and then he said in a quiet, rough voice, "You must rip out the wire fences and plant green living hedges, then things will gradually get better again."

Bläsi and his wife didn't accept that this might be the reason and thought that the old man's advice was extremely foolish. They slaved until grandfather had died, then they sold the neglected farmstead and moved away. They lacked the good sense for grandfather's insight that he had discovered and voiced with the simple wisdom of his old age and experience, which was also lacking in the other farmers nearby. The time was not yet ripe for this here.

At a first superficial glance, it seemed strange that something so insignificant, so long forgotten as uprooting a living hedge should be to blame for the misfortune of these two people. On the other hand, it is not strange that something as wavering and vulnerable as man's well-being can finally be destroyed by seemingly trivial details. The frost only needs to loosen a few stones on the mountain slope and the rock begins to slide over it. A single tear-drop is enough to upset the precious balance. Many other examples can make this obvious in rural life like a valley floor that was sold off and is flooded to build a power station; a clear-cut forest that nobody cared to protect as indispensable; or simply a beautiful group of trees that were naively valued according to their monetary worth. And here it was a living hedge.

APPENDIX

Key facts that everybody who wears cotton should know | The textile industry has a high degree of specialization and typically involves many different production stages. The timescales are also long and factories on several continents engage numerous people in different occupations. Two bioRe® quality labels assure the highest ecological, social and ethical standards.

bioRe® Sustainable Cotton

The highest international standard for organic cotton.

Fair trade cotton with this quality label is sourced from controlled and non-GM organic farms that are managed by smallholders in India and Tanzania. The farmers earn a purchase guarantee for their cotton and a 15% premium on top of the conventional market price. This quality label assures ecologically and ethically sound textile production from cotton cultivation to the yarn. Growing, ginning and spinning the cotton respects the highest social and environmental standards. Textile production is carefully monitored by independent testing agents.

bioRe® Sustainable Textiles

The highest international highest standard for textiles produced from organic cotton.

Fair trade cotton textiles with this quality label are sourced from controlled and non-GM organic smallholders in India and Tanzania. The farmers earn a purchase guarantee for their cotton harvest and remuneration includes a premium of 15% on top of the market price. This quality label guarantees ecologically and ethically sound production from the field to the finished textile. Cotton products are produced without pesticides out of respect for the highest social and environmental standards. The supply chain is 100% transparent and carbon neutral. Each production stage is carefully monitored thanks to the bioRe® control system and independent testing agents. Every garment is re-traceable with a number that identifies each stage of production right back to the farmers.

How can you make a difference as a consumer?

---

1. If possible, you should buy fair trade clothing and keep it for a long time. Remember, recycling old clothes creates new problems.
2. Think about the people who make your clothes with gratitude and kindness. Avoid value judgments such as: "There are worse jobs," or: "They don't know any different." The people who make your clothes are individuals like you and me.
3. When you buy new clothes, choose sustainably produced textiles as often as possible. Several suppliers worldwide offer collections with the bioRe® quality label, an updated list is available here: www.biore.ch/en/style-cases.
4. If you are interested, you can become a member of the bioRe® family by making a donation to the bioRe® Foundation: www.biore-stiftung.ch/en.
5. Take part in the Fashion Revolution, especially the campaign #whomademyclothes, see www.fashionrevolution.org.
6. Get involved in the adventure of long-term relationships. Think of disappointment as a prelude to success.
7. Take heart and join together with others to bring about change.
8. Place your trust in the individual, personal and adventurous possibility that dignity truly exists.

Notes

1 Beckert, Sven: "Empire of Cotton – A Global History", New York, Knopf 2014, p. xvii-xviii.

2 www.keine-gentechnik.de/dossiers/baumwolle-gentechnik.

3 Meier-Rust, Kathrin: "Grosser Unbekannter der Moderne", Neue Zürcher Zeitung, 9 January 2011.

4 Desi is a Sanskrit word that is used in India, Pakistan and Bangladesh. It means 'originating from one's own country or homeland' and forms a contrasting pair with the term 'foreign land'.

5 Hohmann, Patrick: "Werenbachs Uhr", bilgerverlag, Zurich 2015, p. 64.

6 The statistics are from the film "The True Cost" by Andrew Morgan.

Picture Credits

Photo sequence from (left) top to (right) bottom

© Marius Born | front cover, p. 26 [photo 3], 27 [photo 6], 28 [photo 2, 4], 29 [photo 3], 119 [photo 2]
© Joerg Boethling | p. 20, 22 [photo 1, 3, 4], 23 [photo 3, 4], 24 [photo 1, 3], 25, 26 [photo 1, 2], 27 [photo 2], 102f., 104, 105 [photo 2], 121 [photo 1], 140, 152
© bioRe® Foundation | p. 22 [photo 2], 105 [photo 1], 121 [photo 2], 122
© Remo Nägeli | p. 23 [photo 1], 24 [photo 2], 27 [photo 3, 4]
© Till Müllenmeister | p. 23 [photo 2]
© Hans Peter Jost | p. 24 [photo 4], 27 [photo 1], 119 [photo 1], 123 [photo 2]
© Christoph Kaminski | p. 26 [photo 4]
© Remei AG | p. 27 [photo 5,7], 30 [photo 2]
© Utenos | p. 28 [photo 1], p. 29 [photo 2]
© Sainath Ravi | p. 28 [photo 3], 29 [photo 4]
© Georgios Kefalas | p. 29 [photo 1], 70, 120, 123 [photo 1]
© NONOphotography & film | p. 30 [photo 1], 31 [photo 1, 2]
© Patrick Hohmann, private ownership | p. 34, 35, 52, 53, 82f.
© Meinrad Schade | p. 160, portrait of Nicole Müller

Acknowledgement

A life is long, and a book is short. Many of those who influenced the founding of Remei and bioRe® may not have been sufficiently acknowledged here. I would like to thank everyone who has played a part in the adventure of sustainable textiles, working together and sharing the responsibility. Above all, I thank my soulmate, Elisabeth Hohmann Holdener (Dida), my companion and most trusted supporter as well as my children Patrick, Elisabeth (Lisa), Simon and Martin. None of the experiences described in this book would have been thinkable without them.

My sincere thanks also go to:
Mrigendra Jalan, Peter Tschannen, Tadeo Caldas, Jürg and Eliane Peritz, Hans Ueli Loosli, Saro Ratter, Chattobai Somaia, P.V. Rajagopal, Niranjan and Priscilla Pattni, Rajeev and Ritu Baruah, Beat Bernet, Clemens Broer, Armin Holdener, Udo Hermannstorfer, Alfred Egger, Emanuel Büchlin, Simona Matt, K.K. Patodia, Harkishon Udani, Nasor Ali Farai, the late Hilde Mlosch, Roberto Müller, Wolfgang Mahrer, Rolf Schneider, Paul Bischofberger, Julius Reubke, Margrit Hugentobler, Judith Schuler Schmuki as well as the new generation who has embraced the idea: Marion Röttges and my son Simon Hohmann, Christa Suter, Markus Kunz, Philipp Wyss, Pia Bracher, Marco Paul, Charles Mabuga, Vivek Rawal, and all past and present employees of Remei, the bioRe® Foundation, bioRe® Tanzania Ltd., bioRe® Foundation Tanzania, bioRe® India Ltd. as well as bioRe® India Association and everybody whom I cannot begin to thank by listing their names. However, they all made a vital

contribution in the spirit of the inscription at the entrance to the bioRe® India Training Centre:

"A healthy social life is found only when, in the mirror of each soul, the whole community finds its reflection, and when, in the whole community, the virtue of each one is living." Rudolf Steiner

Special thanks go to the director Nino Jacusso whose film "Fair Traders" vividly conveyed hope to young people that has encouraged me throughout my life: namely, that we make friends with people of different cultures and can create something together with them, so that they have a dignified life with a sensible occupation.

My warmest thanks also go to the author Nicole Müller who listened for many hours to my life stories, who experienced Tanzania and India with me and whose sensitive and sympathetic words describe my eventful life and who inspired me to publish this book.

And last but not least, my sincere gratitude goes to the publisher Anne Rüffer and her team, especially Saskia Nobir, who have accepted and wonderfully produced this book.

In gratitude
Patrick Hohmann

About the author

Nicole Müller, (b. 1962 in Basel) is a writer, publicist and consultant. She studied Romance studies and Russian in Zurich, Paris and Bochum. Her long-standing expertise in communications was recognized in 2007 with a Swiss and international diploma in marketing communications. Her literary work includes the novels "Denn das ist das Schreckliche an der Liebe", "Mehr am 15. September", "Kaufen!" as well as a biography about Annemarie Schwarzenbach. Nicole Müller became well known as a moderator of "Sternstunde Philosophie". As a consultant for brand management and communications she has advised clients such as Globus, UNICEF, Swiss Re, Credit Suisse, Hilti Foundation and Sonnmatt Luzern.

OTHER BOOKS IN THIS SERIES

rüffer & rub visionaries

Johannes Dieterich, Ed.

**Tony Rinaudo –
The Forestmaker**

Paperback (english)
ISBN 978-3-906304-43-4
Available as ebook.

Alternative
Nobel Prize
2018

The Australian agronomist Tony Rinaudo revolutionized reforestation in Africa with Farmer Managed Natural Regeneration (FMNR). His method is based on deploying tree stumps and roots that still grow even in degraded landscapes: thanks to the protection and care of the shoots, the original tree population can be regenerated without major financial costs. The method is now successfully applied in at least 24 African countries. Where the desert was still expanding 20 years ago, farmers reforest large areas with FMNR: in Niger alone seven million hectares of land were already restored in this way.

With articles from Johannes Dieterich, Tony Rinaudo, Dennis Garrity, and an interview with Günter Nooke.

Ernst Bromeis

Every drop counts
Swimming for the right to water

Brochure
ISBN 978-3-906304-23-6

Water is the basis for life on this planet. It is required by human beings, animals and the rest of nature. But this basis is becoming more and more endangered – by pollution, by global warming and by wasteful consumption in households. This is making water more and more valuable. That is why international corporations are purchasing rights to water. Switzerland is considering allowing hydraulic power plants to be sold to Chinese companies.

Ernst Bromeis' objective is to make us aware that water is not unlimited in availability. Large corporations are not to be allowed to exploit sources of groundwater in ways preventing human beings from having access to water, or forcing them to consume unclean water. To realize these objectives, Ernst Bromeis undertakes spectacular athletic deeds. Among these: in 2008, he swam across 200 lakes located in Switzerland's canton of Graubünden. In 2104, he swam the 1.247 kilometers of the Rhine, which starts in Lago di Dentro and ends in the North Sea.

Hans R. Herren

How to Nourish the world

Brochure
ISBN 978-3-906304-25-0

“A world with sufficient and healthful food for all, food produced by healthy people living and working in a healthy environment” is the vision of Hans Rudolf Herren and his Biovision foundation.

The foundation has dedicated itself to the development, dissemination and application of ecological methods of farming in Africa. The focus of its work is the processing and hands-on distribution and exchanging of information. This is being undertaken to enable people in Kenya, Uganda, Tanzania and Egypt’s acting on their own and in the interests of themselves and the environment. The foundation’s projects include the prevention of malaria and the fostering of income through the cultivation of medicinal plants. These projects improve the conditions of life for local residents, and serve as role models for training programs.

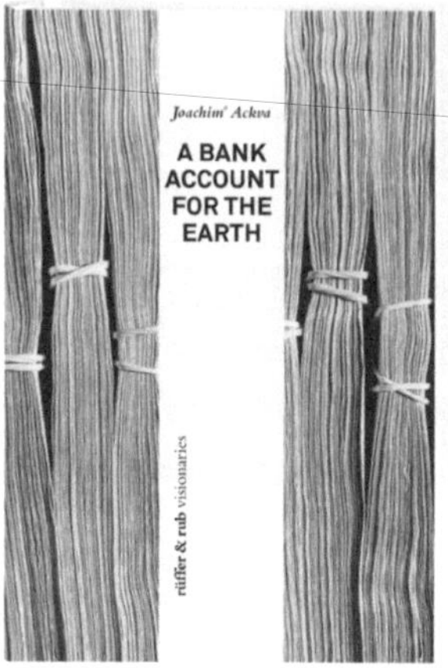

Joachim° Ackva

A bank account for the earth

Paperback
ISBN 978-3-906304-24-3

Humanity is facing major challenges. Achieving peace in a world spending more on armaments than even in the Cold War era. Imparting prosperity to the billions so far from it. Saving a world economy from drowning in debt. Preserving nature in an era in which the populations of those animals that constitute the bases of our ecosystems have been halved since 1970.

To overcome these challenges, Joachim° Ackva is calling upon each person on this planet to pay a sum equal to one thousandth of her or his net assets into the Planetary Bank Account, which is to be administered by the UN's Secretariat. These funds will go to decisively advance the achievement of the UN's Global Goals.